Nonlegal Careers for Lawyers

NONLEGAL CAREERS FOR LAWYERS
In the Private Sector

Second Edition

Frances Utley with Gary A. Munneke

American Bar Association
Law Student Division
Section of Economics of Law Practice
Standing Committee on Professional Utilization and
Career Development

Library of Congress Catalog Card Number 83-73457
ISBN: 0-89707-129-8

American Bar Association
750 North Lake Shore Drive
Chicago, Illinois 60611

Produced by the ABA Press.

2 3 4 5 6 7 87 86 85 84

Foreword

The second edition of *Nonlegal Careers for Lawyers: In the Private Sector* by Frances Utley with Gary A. Munneke is an update of the popular 1980 monograph *Nonlegal Careers: New Opportunities for Lawyers*, produced by the Standing Committee on Professional Utilization and Career Development of the American Bar Association. In the Foreword to the earlier edition the Standing Committee said:

> For some time now lawyers have been finding new and interesting ways to utilize the skills acquired with legal training in various opportunities within business and industry. As these fields may present challenging career opportunities for you as well, the Standing Committee on Professional Utilization and Career Development of the American Bar Association has sponsored the preparation of this book and supervised its editorial content.

The second edition takes into account an increasing recognition on the part of law students, counselors, and the bar that nonlegal careers are legitimate pursuits for lawyers, a development precipitated at least in part by publication of the first edition. This edition also covers areas which were left out of the original monograph, and the result is a larger, more comprehensive book.

The second edition, moreover, has been incorporated in the ABA Career Series, a joint effort of the Standing Committee on Professional Utilization and Career Development, the Section of Economics of Law Practice, and the Law Student Division. The Career Series is intended ultimately to produce a wide range of books on a variety of careers for lawyers.

The Steering Committee, comprised of Gary A. Munneke, chairman, for the Standing Committee, Theodore Orenstein for the Section, and William D. Henslee for the Division, wishes to thank and acknowledge ABA Staff Liaison to the Standing Committee, Frances Utley, for her work as author of *Nonlegal Careers*. It should be noted that while she was primarily responsible for writing the first edition, her name does not appear anywhere in that publication. Although the Steering Committee wanted to recognize the earlier work of the Standing Committee, it now also desires to give credit to Frances Utley for her contribution.

Gary A. Munneke, Chairman
ABA Career Series Steering Committee

Contents

PART 3: WHAT ARE THE POSSIBILITIES WITH ASSOCIATIONS AND OTHER ORGANIZATIONS?

PART 4: HOW TO FIND AND GET A NONLEGAL POSITION

PART 5: RESOURCES

Introduction

Many law students have graduated with the disquieting feeling that the traditional practice of law was not the career choice they had envisioned when they started their law school training. Others have realized a mistaken choice after a few years in practice. Very often these individuals have been reluctant to move away from traditional practice, assuming that moving into a nonlegal career was opting for a second-rate choice.

These feelings have all too often been magnified by family and friends unfamiliar with the many alternatives available to lawyers today. Yet there are lawyer corporation presidents, lawyer doctors, lawyer hockey players, lawyer sportscasters, and lawyer actors and actresses, to name but a few.

This book, however, is not about that rare individual or two who may have achieved fame in a nonlegal occupation and who also happens to be a lawyer. This book is about nonlegal careers that are realistically attainable by those whose legal training provides a leg up in career advancement in the business world. The positions presented are at the starting level or are early advancement points which afford opportunities to attain even higher positions later. Not one is presented as a second choice or a dead end in terms of its potential.

You will note, however, that these nonlegal careers have a special appeal to legally trained persons who have other areas of training or experience. If you are one of these individuals, your legal training expands your career potential dramatically because you now offer a new area of skill that has dozens of applications in your chosen field.

What is the magic of a legal education that should broaden career potential not only for individuals specialized in another field, but also for the new lawyer who simply knows that traditional law practice is not for him or her?

The magic is that, even if you failed to realize it at the time, you acquired three basic skills in law school that are not provided by any other part of our educational system. One skill or another may be emphasized in other areas, but the combination of the three is only really provided by legal training.

The first skill is the ease with which you now deal with legal terminology and legal concepts. Just as the law touches the life of almost every individual today, so it touches every business enterprise. For example, the organization you work for enters into a contract with another. How many of your fellow workers will be able to read that contract and understand what must be done to comply with its terms? New legislation is pending which will impact on your organization. Others may note the same legislation and be unable to define its potential effect because they don't understand the language. Yet this language has become second nature to you.

The second skill you have acquired is that of analyzing facts. Don't take this skill for granted. It was pounded into you in three or four years of law school training until you do it automatically. Yet it is a skill that applies itself easily to all types of problems, not just legal cases. It is not a common skill as you will discover when you deal not only with persons who can see the forest, but not the trees, but also with others who can see the trees but not the forest.

The third skill is that of persuading others of the rightness of your conclusions. This skill increases in value as you move upward in the business world. At the outset you will undoubtedly be receiving orders and information. As you progress you will be giving orders and information. The better able you are to persuade others to your point of view or suggested course of action, the greater your chance of success with your project or idea.

These three skills are not only basic to your value in a nonlegal position, but they are also fundamental to obtaining your entry into the business world. This book will show you how to use these points to best advantage in obtaining the position you want.

If you are just beginning to think about an alternative career to the traditional practice of law, however, you probably feel uncertain as to just where to start. This uncertainty is understandable. The number of choices open to you is virtually limitless. In fact, judging from the experience of those who have chosen this career path before you, the choice is limited only by your imagination and your selected career goals.

To help you select the direction of your career planning and start you off with your first position toward those goals, this book will suggest broad areas of nonlegal work in which lawyers are currently employed. As you read, keep asking yourself such questions as "Would this type of work interest me?" "Would I be good at this type of work?" "If I started at this point, what might my future plans and development include?"

Once you have selected two or three areas that appear promising to you based on your gut reaction alone, you can begin to develop more information and depth in your search. Until you reach a final decision, however, keep an open mind. The whole range of nonlegal careers for lawyers is developing so rapidly as they prove attractive to lawyers for professional satisfaction and opportunities for development that new potentialities may develop even as you are exploring current possibilities open to you.

While this book is aimed at helping you get started in the development of a nonlegal career, it does not touch on similar possibilities that exist in the government at all levels nor the career development techniques unique to that area. A later book in the Career Series *Nonlegal Careers for Lawyers: In the Public Sector* will deal with nonlegal government work.

1
Considerations in a Nonlegal Career

Pros and Cons of a Nonlegal Career

One of the inescapable facts of any career decision is that it will have both its pros and its cons. Since your needs, interests, and abilities will not duplicate those of any other person, it is vitally important that you give careful consideration to all the factors that might bear upon the success of your final decision.

One important consideration may be that you already find business administration and management interesting and challenging, and this discovery may be the single biggest motivation toward your deciding on a nonlegal business management career.

Another consideration is the sheer number of possibilities open to you, as well as the evidence that the number can be expected to increase in the future. Obviously there is considerable opportunity here. There is a finite number of law offices, corporate legal departments, and government legal departments. American ingenuity has created an almost infinite number of organizations where legal knowledge has effective application. Even beyond that fact, there is the potential for you as an entrepreneur. This range of choice gives you the maximum possibility for matching your particular talents and skills to specific opportunities. This fact in turn increases your chance for maximum career satisfaction.

A third consideration is the fact that the skills you acquire in nonlegal positions can be transferred far more easily to new geographic areas than can the skills of practicing lawyers for whom bar admission requirements provide an inhibiting factor to easy relocation.

If you wish to confine your job search now to a specific geographic area, the increase in the total number of possibilities may work to your advantage. As you look to the future, the existence of geographic flexibility may be important to meet your personal plans and needs.

The final consideration may be even more difficult to assess simply because it involves looking into the future and projecting your anticipated needs and desires, and then balancing them against possible future developments within the professional fields you are considering, including the traditional legal profession.

At the outset comes the decision as to whether you wish to be admitted to the bar. In most nonlegal positions, as you have undoubtedly noted, such admission is not essential to the full utilization of skills you have already acquired from law school training. On the other hand, admission might be important for future promotion because of additional functions you might perform. There is no easy answer to this question, nor is there likely to be one in the foreseeable future; but from the standpoint of flexibility, bar admission will be a definite advantage for you.

The answer to the question of admission to the bar will not only lie within the business community itself and your hoped-for development within that community, but the answer may be affected as well by future developments within the legal profession. Already there is experimentation with the certification of specialists and recertification based upon experience and the completion of continuing legal education courses to qualify for practice. How may these changes impact on your business management career if you are not involved in the actual practice of law?

So the law school graduate who chooses not to practice law must recognize the strong possibility that it will be virtually impossible after a few years to second guess his or her decision on a business management career as opposed to a legal career.

The reason is essentially an economic one. To see why this is so, consider a hypothetical situation. You enter the traffic department of a corporation as a management trainee. At the same time another graduate of your class enters the legal department of the same company. You will be provided highly specialized training in traffic department procedures, problems, and policies. As your experience grows you will receive greater responsibilities and you will probably be using your legal training to enhance your job performance. As your effectiveness increases with knowledge and experience, you will be receiving merit increases of salary.

At the same time your contemporary in the legal department will also be receiving specialized training in lawyer practice skills. Again, the company will expect that as his or her knowledge and experience increase, advances in income will result. At the end of five years each of you will essentially be specialists, you in the traffic area and your fellow graduate in the legal practice area. Both of you are performing much-needed services for the organization.

At that point suppose the two of you were to exchange positions. You would be the neophyte lawyer and your colleague the novice traffic specialist. It simply would not make economic sense for the company to continue to pay either of you at the higher salary level you had achieved when the skills acquired in the previous position could not be fully utilized in the new one. From your point of view the question would simply be, Can I afford to start over again at a beginner's salary? Most people answer no.

This does not mean that lawyers in nonlegal positions *never* move into the legal ones, only that it is extremely difficult to do so and thus the move seldom occurs.

Because the choice of whether to pursue a nonlegal career is a major one, it deserves your most thoughtful consideration. Even at the start your choice will determine the approach you take to the marketplace for your abilities.

Choosing a Nonlegal Career

by Gary A. Munneke

(This section, with minor alterations, first appeared in *Barrister* magazine, © 1981, under the title "Is Your Career on Target?" Used with permission.)

For George, the thought of getting up each morning and going to work was almost unbearable. His job lacked meaning; there was no personal satisfaction in the work he did, no incentive to perform well. There was no future. Like many thousands of other lawyers each year, George was rebelling by seeking a new career. What set him apart from other attorneys was that he had been a partner with the same prominent law firm for the last 25 years. Many lawyers would have given anything to have George's job, or even to work for George's firm.

Sally, after graduating from law school, had spent months interviewing for a job without success. She finally found a sole practitioner who needed an associate. Sally got paid a percentage of the fees she billed, a livelihood that fell far short of her law school expectations. And she felt that her work could have been done by an average third-grader. So Sally was moving on too.

These are two cases from the files of a career counselor, but they are not unusual. Although many lawyers are challenged and satisfied with their work, many others are frustrated and unhappy. Some, like George and Sally, are turning away from traditional legal careers; too many other attorneys suffer in silence.

There is a myth in the legal profession that lawyers keep one job throughout their legal careers. If this myth ever was true, which is debatable, it certainly is not today. The average lawyer will hold 5 to 8 jobs in the 40 years between law school graduation and retirement, and a high percentage of attorneys will make at least one major career change in their lives.

Evidence of rampant job dissatisfaction is easy to find, from Johnny Paycheck's hit song "Take This Job and Shove It" to Johnny Carson's complaints to NBC that the lack of challenge—and not money—prompts him to consider employment elsewhere. Studs Terkel, a lawyer himself, suggests in his book *Working* that job dissatisfaction is pervasive in our society. People don't seem to be happy in their present positions; they are all on the road to somewhere and just passing time in their present jobs.

It is clear that lawyers are not alone. It would be unwise, however, to assume that dissatisfaction in the legal profession is totally a product of our changing times, sunspot activity, or some other global witchcraft.

In many ways the legal profession is unique. The dissatisfaction of lawyers with their professional lives can be explained, if not totally understood. One answer to the problem of job dissatisfaction may lie in the kinds of alternatives to the practice of law that will be described later. A caveat is in order, however: dissatisfaction is the stuff that progress is made of, that careers grow on, that futures are built with. Find a man or woman who is completely happy in a job and you will find someone who has no dreams. Each of us is, in one sense, always in the job market. There are very few who would not leave what they are doing for some golden opportunity.

John L. Holland, one of America's foremost career theorists, explains that high levels of job dissatisfaction, or "dissonance" as he calls it, usually produce one of three responses: to change ourselves, to change our environment, or to leave the environment. When we change ourselves we accept whatever it was that was bothering us. When we change the environment we eliminate the offending problem. If we can't do that, we look for something new. For instance, if a lawyer is told he will not be made a partner in his law firm but can stay as an associate, he will either accept the decision, attempt to prove that he should be made partner, or pull out an old resume and start to revise it.

Career decisions are almost always complex ones involving many considerations. Factors such as the employability of the individual in the marketplace, tolerance for the bad situation, willingness to assume a risk, and the need for security inevitably weigh heavily in the equation. Every year thousands of lawyers change jobs. For many of them the transition is smooth, but often the change is difficult and painful. Sometimes it is destructive.

What are the roots of lawyer dissatisfaction? The Young Lawyers Division sponsored two seminars titled "The Job Changers" in 1983. Participants at these programs, led by career counselors from law schools in the National Association for Law Placement (NALP), reported a number of reasons for wanting to change jobs. The most commonly named was that their present employment did not utilize the skills they believed they possessed as lawyers. It is important to note that most of these people held legal jobs at the time the seminars were held. A second reason for dissatisfaction was low salary and a perception that the position had no future, or both. A third complaint was of unpleasant working conditions, including conflicts with supervising attorneys.

These indications of the reason for dissatisfaction differ from those reported in a survey by the California Young Lawyers Association. The CYLA study uses the term *underemployed* to apply to the lawyer who: (1) is practicing law and does not have enough legal work to stay busy full time, or (2) is employed in a nonlegal position because he or she has been unable to obtain a legal one.

The term underemployment is simply too subjective to be useful in discussing job dissatisfaction. How many lawyers would call themselves underemployed in jobs others would consider ideal? How many of those without enough legal work do not operate an efficient law office, or have not learned to attract and keep clients?

The preceding questions are not intended to criticize the California study but rather to focus attention on specific job-related factors that have a major bearing on whether one will be happy in a job or seek a new one. The three reasons articulated by participants in the Job Changers programs focus on situations where a lawyer would be willing to make a job change whether he is in a legal or nonlegal job.

The first complaint — not using the skills one possesses or learns in law school — is most critical. Holland, in *Making Vocational Choices*, presents the theory that individuals tend to like what they succeed at, and that they will succeed in the future in activities utilizing the same skills and activities they have succeeded at in the past. In other words, career changing ought to involve careful evaluation of past job behavior to determine competencies that will most likely produce success in a new situation.

Having the feeling a job contributes to a positive direction in one's career is essential to self-concept and job satisfaction. Jobs perceived as dead ends or as unchallenging usually become former jobs of employees who can neither change them nor accept the status quo. Salary can influence whether a job is considered to have a future. In these times of rapid inflation, a low-paying but rewarding job is more likely to be perceived as lacking a future. There is evidence that the median income of lawyers is dropping, and although this drop can be attributed partly to the large increase in the number of new lawyers who are at the low end of the pay scale, it appears likely that the lawyer with the average salary is not winning the fight against inflation. Advertisements offering cut-rate legal fees and increased competition have not helped attorneys in this fight.

Working conditions are another factor often mentioned in lawyers' decisions to leave their jobs. Everything else may be fine, but if you hate your co-workers, your clients, or your surroundings, you have to go. Psychologist and Yale Law School teacher Dr. Robert Redmount, speaking to the annual meeting of NALP, suggested that the legal profession on the whole abandons humanistic values in treatment of lawyer employees, and that concern for the individual's job satisfaction and career development is often neglected. Whatever the reasons for job dissatisfaction, it is undeniable that it is common and frustrating to the lawyer who experiences it, particularly if he does not know where to turn. This need not be so.

The number of careers open to persons trained in the law is virtually unlimited. There are legal considerations in every form of human endeavor in this complex world. Even when the work cannot be said to constitute practicing law in the sense of giving legal advice to clients, a lawyer working in a field outside the law will be dealing with the interface of the law and that field. Legal skills undoubtedly give the lawyer a much better ability to manage this interface than the nonlawyer.

In a broader sense, it is probably true that such legal skills as spotting issues, analyzing problems, conducting research, and persuading others can be useful in almost every job. However, A. Kenneth Pye, chancellor of Duke University and former Duke Law School dean, in his article "Meeting the Needs for Legal Education in the South" wrote, "In one sense, society's need for lawyers is immaterial to the issue of whether more lawyers should be educated. Those who regard law as a humanistic discipline will find value in educating all who are qualified without regard to the vocation they will ultimately pursue. The vast majority of law students go to law school because they desire to practice law. . . . [H]owever, relatively few people go to law school for the purpose of broadening their perspective on life or as a general background for other ventures. . . . To train lawyers to fill positions which can be adequately performed by persons with bachelor's or master's degrees is a misuse of resources. . . ."

Pye understands that most people do not go to law school with the expectation that they will do something totally unrelated to law. Projections of the annual NALP Employment Survey, the 1971 Lawyer Statistical Report, and the U.S. Department of Labor, Bureau of Labor Statistics, all confirm that the majority of law graduates and lawyers enter and continue to practice law throughout their careers. Private law, corporate, government, and legal services practice account for the bulk of the bar, although there are a number of other groups such as military, labor union, educational institution, and public interest lawyers. All these people usually must be licensed to do what they do: go to court, give legal advice, prepare legal instruments, and negotiate legal agreements.

Lawyers whose activites do not constitute practicing law are often described as working in nontraditional or alternative careers. Such terminology is unfortunate because it implies that these positions are second-rate. NALP has undertaken a massive study of these areas called the Career Options Project, leaving the nonlegal and law-related work to be described simply as options. NALP plans to prepare materials on a wide array of career options for prelaw students, law students, and lawyers.

The 1978 NALP Employment Survey identified 105 nonlegal jobs accepted by law graduates. The opportunities described are as real for the career changer as for the recent graduate. Those who wonder if law practice will be satisfying for them, or who no longer feel excited about their legal jobs should ask the question: Can my skills be better used in a different field? If so, it might be time to consider something new.

Nonlegal positions for lawyers may be in a variety of organizational settings. Many are in business and industry, at all levels of the corporate structure. They are in government—federal, state, local, and multinational. Some are in quasi-governmental private associations or corporations. Many positions are in private associations, including professional organizations. They are in educational institutions, both public and private. In some instances the jobs discussed below will be unique to one area such as corporations; in others they will be found in varied organizational settings.

Administration and Management. Business administration and management provide a variety of opportunities for attorneys. These positions may be found in corporations, in government at all levels, and in private associations. In large corporate concerns there are often formal in-house training programs. The trend in business today, however, is for the small business to hire a lawyer/manager. Organizations attempting to reduce skyrocketing legal expenses but not large enough to consider developing an in-house legal department, often seek lawyers with some business experience to fill management positions that have limited legal advisory functions. Banks, insurance companies, industrial companies, and other businesses will consider individuals trained in law who have a background in or demonstrate a facility for managerial work. There is an old adage that you can always teach business to a JD but you will never teach law to an MBA. Management or public administration posts in government are often filled by lawyers, as are positions as managers and directors of many private associations. This last group includes bar associations and law firms.

Money Management. When one thinks of money management, banks and accounting firms come to mind. Commercial banking and public accounting have attracted many qualified lawyers over the years. Accounting firms frequently recruit alongside law firms at law schools, though partnerships in CPA firms are restricted to holders of the CPA certificate. It is possible, however, to complete the CPA requirements after graduating from law school. Banks frequently hire lawyers to work in their trust departments, and assignment to commercial banking is also a possibility. Brokerage houses and investment firms have been known to employ lawyers, although this is a less common practice than with banks and accounting firms. Fund-raising positions, which often involve coordinating deferred giving programs, are filled from time to time with lawyers, especially those with experience in estate or trust work. Fund raising takes place in the corporate setting, the educational institution, the private foundation, and the political area.

Planning, Organization. Planners are found everywhere, although it is not always possible to tell where they have been after they leave. Systems analysis and professional consulting call for considerate expertise in the substantive professional area. The legal problems faced by planners attempting to integrate new ideas into existing systems make legally trained persons valuable in this area. While many planning positions are in the public sector, there also are opportunities in the private sector.

Insurance. Insurance is in a separate category because it is such a large industry. Positions for lawyers outside the general counsel's office are primarily in three areas: sales, plan management, and claims adjustment. Insurance sales can be lucrative work, but it is not a job for everyone. A number of insurance companies recruit attorneys as sales representatives to handle complex benefit plans and insurance programs for corporations, partnerships, and professionals. Plan management is a term intended to describe everything done by the insurance company in its home or branch offices to administer its accounts. Claims adjustment is perhaps the least euphemistic of the job titles used. These positions have in the past by themselves provided limited future opportunities for lawyers, although claims work can be a stepping stone to other opportunities in the company.

Administration of Justice. Most lawyers view the judicial system as comprised mainly of lawyers and judges. There are, however, a great many opportunities for lawyers who do not practice law in the justice system. Judicial administration includes court administration—such positions as permanent court clerks, administrators, and court reporters. It also includes the broader area of criminal justice administration. There are lawyers involved at almost every level in positions other than as advocates. Prison or parole administration may require other specialized training than that provided by law school, but fields such as law enforcement do not.

Numerous police departments use in-house legal advisors who educate officers on legal issues. Some law graduates go into law enforcement as officers or agents, for example with the FBI. Private investigation is a related field, and there are actually a few lawyers around who find it more exciting and rewarding to be Paul Drake than to be Perry Mason.

Real Estate. Many lawyers enter real estate after years of practicing law when they realize that their clients are making all the money. Some lawyers make the change gradually, others just quit their law practices. Real estate sales and development are two highly visible fields, and both involve highly risky and highly competitive but potentially lucrative work. Less visible are title companies. It is ironic that in many states practicing lawyers have complained that title companies have stolen their business, and now title insurance companies are being taken over by lawyers. Another growing career area in a world of limited energy is mineral land management and petroleum land management.

Legislative Work. Legislatures, on all levels, number more member lawyers than any other professional group. The same is true of their aids, research assistants, and paid campaigners. Former legislators and lawyers often become involved in lobbying for the multitude of organizations trying to influence legislation. Need more be said?

Communications. The skills of lawyering (writing, speaking, persuading) are the same skills required of individuals in the communications field. Some of the areas where lawyers have been successful are writing, publishing, broadcast and print journalism, acting, filmmaking, advertising, and public relations. While communications careers are attractive to many people, the opportunities are limited, and a strong background in the communications field or personal contacts along with some good luck will undoubtedly be necessary for one to break into the field.

Educational and Academic Positions. A vast area of opportunity for lawyers is in education and education-related pursuits. While educational positions are not likely to be high paying, the freedom and creativity fostered in the educational setting combine strongly to attract many lawyers. Teaching positions immediately come to mind — not only in law schools but also in universities, community colleges, and secondary schools — in legal subjects as well as others. Competition for the most prestigious teaching jobs is keen, and increasingly practical experience after law school is required.

Administrators, who may or may not be teachers, or may or may not be in law school, are involved in such varied responsibilities as student personnel administration, placement, admissions, financial aid, alumni affairs, academic counseling, and Continuing Legal Education (CLE). The CLE field has grown dramatically since the early 1970s, with practically every law school and bar association as well as many private oganizations getting into the act. If mandatory CLE for lawyers ever becomes a reality throughout the nation, CLE jobs will become even more common.

Education also includes librarianships and research and publishing jobs. Law librarians who possess a JD and a master of library science degree can find work in any of the country's law schools, in many courts and government offices, and in an increasing number of law firms. Professional research groups and law book publishers round out the academic positions.

A discussion of career alternatives for lawyers would not be complete without mentioning the entrepreneurs. There are countless stories of lawyers who have entered business on their own and succeeded. Perhaps it is the tradition of hanging out a shingle or the independent nature of many who choose to go to law school. Perhaps it is the recognition of opportunities or contacts made during years of practicing law. Whatever the reasons, there are enough lawyers who strike out in business on their own that the possibility should be mentioned to potential career changers.

This account has given a quick overview of some of the careers pursued by lawyers who don't practice law. It should be remembered that one lawyer's meat is another's poison, and all these jobs will not appeal to everyone. People who work in these areas do so because they want to and not because they have to. Nonlegal jobs provide a future for the Georges and Sallys of the legal profession who are searching outside the conventional practice of law.

(Many of the jobs described in this chapter are discussed in greater detail in the remaining chapters of this book. Others will be covered in the companion volume, Nonlegal Careers for Lawyers: In the Public Sector.*)*

Relationships with the Legal Department

How are the relationships between legally trained persons in nonlegal positions and members of the in-house law department? Good, and getting better every year. Understanding some of the reasons for that answer can be of assistance in shaping your own business management career. While the same principles apply to government and other types of organizations, the corporate experience has been the most obvious and so the easiest area in which to define how these relationships operate.

Corporate in-house law departments are a fairly recent development within the legal profession, and in the last thirty years they have represented the fastest growing segment of the profession. As with any new development, the early years were spent in defining roles and responsibilities. The employment of legally trained persons in nonlegal activities within the corporate body is even more recent.

Today the corporate legal department is in reality an independent law office serving the needs of a single client. The basic function of the department is to delineate the legal boundaries within which the management of the corporation is free to exercise its ingenuity in successfully managing the corporate enterprise. At the same time corporate lawyers seek to find ways legally to achieve proper corporate objectives. The proximity of the department to corporate activity and management has enabled it to practice preventive law in a way simply not possible by outside counsel.

Over the years, however, corporations have grown more complex in structure, and government regulatory activities have grown by leaps and bounds. As a consequence, the corporate legal department increasingly has found it difficult to keep on top of every potential problem area.

Several years ago a general counsel wrote a tongue in cheek article for a professional publication on how to develop a "spy system" that would bring possible difficulties to the attention of the legal department. Essentially the problem faced by the corporate lawyers was that of the entire profession, How do you get laymen to recognize those potential legal problems?

It has become apparent that by having legally trained persons scattered widely throughout the administrative and managerial activities of the corporation this basic difficulty can be solved. There remained, however, a question as to whether these persons would perceive themselves in cooperation or in conflict with the members of the legal department. As more and more legally trained persons enter business management careers, the answer to that second question is evolving. Perhaps because they have consciously chosen a career other than the practice of law and possibly because spotting potential legal hazards is only a part of their duties and responsibilities, the potential conflicts are simply failing to develop.

Of course there may be individual personality differences, and corporate lines of communication at times may be faulty. Taken as a whole, however, the relationship between the two groups can only be characterized as good, and getting better every year.

What the Employer Needs and the Skills You Offer

Applicants for positions may feel that the qualities the employer is looking for represent some sort of an impenetrable mystery. This simply is not so. An understanding of the qualifications required for any position can be reached with a little imagination and some practice. You should be able to analyze the requirements for any position in which you might be interested by asking only four basic questions.

1. *Are any specific technical skills required?* For example, it seems probable that an accounting undergraduate degree would be necessary in the financial area. Ability to understand the terminology of a contract would probably be necessary in the contract administration field.

Are there any skills which might be acceptable substitutes for the specified technical skills? Are there related skills which might enhance job performance? Perhaps you are interested in real estate. With a little thought you can see how legal training might provide basic skills that would be useful in your work, but also you should imagine the enhancement of those skills if you happen to have concentrated your studies in real estate and related fields.

Carrying the analysis one step further is extremely important where no specific technical skills appear to be required. By analyzing your own experience and training, you can pinpoint those skills you have acquired which would put you ahead of the competition. It may also serve to eliminate consideration of posts for which you do not have the necessary technical background.

2. *What degree of educational development is required for satisfactory job performance?* When a business organization is seeking to employ someone for its legal department, it is obvious that a law degree will be required simply because it is basic to bar admission. Very seldom, indeed, will nonlegal positions specifically call for a law degree. It will be your task to figure out *why a law degree better qualifies you for the position* than any other which may be specified, as well

as why a law degree better qualifies you for the position than any other applicant for that position. In the Resources section of this book you will find listings of specific positions. Use them to practice deciding if a law degree is a particular job qualification.

The preceding point is not to be sloughed off lightly. In *From Law Student to Lawyer: A Career Planning Manual,* the first book in the Career Series, you will find suggestions on analyzing your skills that will be of help in this step. If the company has not defined the position in terms of a law degree, then it is to your competitive advantage to be able to point out why the skills of a person possessing such a degree will contribute substantially to effective job performance. In the later section of this book on conducting a job search in nonlegal areas you will find suggestions on how to make this point.

3. *What personality qualities are required, and what are desirable?* Assume from the outset that every organization is seeking the most intelligent and highly motivated people it can find, and that the requirements are tremendously important at the administrative and managerial levels. Assume also that leadership potential and the ability to work effectively with others will also be prime considerations. In addition, you must define what additional qualities might contribute most effectively to success in the particular area under consideration. Some of the intangible characteristics employers look for which you will want to demonstrate include:

Initiative	Adaptability	Decisiveness
Planning	Versatility	Articulateness
Creativity	Concentration	

All of these are good qualities, and each would contribute to successful job performance. At this point, however, what you seek to do is to isolate those traits that would be *most* conducive to performance in a specific area. For example, you might expect that greater originality and creativity would be demanded in the marketing function than in contract administration. As you analyze your own personal strengths against the probable qualities needed in the area that you are considering, you will be able to judge better its congeniality to you and also to assess your competitive stature as a candidate against other possible applicants for the position.

4. *What is the degree of industry knowledge and procedural know-how that will be required to successfully fill the demands of the posi-*

tion? If you are just entering the business world, the employer may not expect you to have this knowledge. It is not something that you can learn by taking certain prescribed courses while in school. It is acquired only by experience on the job.

The importance of this last question to you as you begin a business career is that it defines the type of position which you will be seeking. The most frequent title given to this post in the corporate world is management trainee which, as the title indicates, is precisely what will happen. You will be trained by management in the industry knowledge and procedural know-how you will be required to have to perform in more advanced positions. While government or other organizations may not use this term but some such word as *intern,* the general principle of learning the business on the job still applies.

In a few industries there are specific titles for entry level positions, such as claims adjustor in the insurance industry. The phrase "entry level or management trainee type of position," however, is likely to lessen the chance of misunderstanding due to semantic confusion.

In answering the four questions considered above, you will naturally want to assess the special qualifications that your legal training enables you to bring to the position. These include the following:

The first and most obvious one is your knowledge of legal terminology and its interpretations. For example, how can you possibly monitor contract performance if you can't read and understand what the contract requires? Having that knowledge has served to place many legally trained persons in nonlegal positions.

The second ability is more subtle. It involves the honing of your analytical ability, "learning to think like a lawyer."

Murphy's law, "If anything can possibly go wrong, it will," is a familiar one in the business community. The ability to anaylze problems and suggest remedies is a highly valued skill. Furthermore, it is a skill not easily acquired, as no doubt your own painful memories will attest. Your analytical skill does not lose its value simply by being translated into a different context.

The third skill which you have acquired through law school training is persuasiveness. Essentially the skill involves the marshaling of your facts in a logical and orderly manner to persuade the particular audience being addressed as to the soundness of your conclusions. In any given situation you will have a number of facts and supporting data. Consider how differently you would present those facts and data to a client whom you were counseling, as defense attorney in a jury trial, or in an appellate brief. This persuasive skill is just as valuable in the business community because of its almost unlimited usefulness.

The key words in the employer's lexicon are "productivity" and "profitability." The success with which you answer the four questions raised in this chapter determine the extent to which you are speaking the employer's language.

2

What Are the Possibilities in Business Organizations?

Lawyers Choose Nonlegal Business Careers

In most large corporations the number of legally trained persons employed in administrative and management posts far exceeds that of the legal department. This was the finding of the Standing Committee on Professional Utilization and Career Development of the American Bar Association in a survey of over 60 of the nation's largest corporations.

Survey responses indicated there were several reasons for this phenomenon.

These individuals in nonlegal posts had consciously opted for a career in business management rather than the traditional practice of law.

Legal training was viewed as a valuable tool to upgrade job performance. In fact, a substantial number of these persons had obtained their legal training while on the job, and in a few instances the company felt that legal training was so important to job performance that it had underwritten the cost of law school education for promising employees.

In some of the companies, management experience was essential if the individual was to receive consideration for top executive posts, and some of the individuals had transferred from the legal department specifically in order to acquire this experience.

The very diversity of corporate positions held by those with legal training gives solid evidence of the vast range of opportunity open to those who decide that a career in business management is more compatible with their interests and abilities than traditional practice. If you are one of these, you will want to know something about what legally trained persons are presently doing within their corporations and businesses, and what areas are relatively unexplored as yet.

Because of the diversity of corporate structures, the various jobs described are grouped by function rather than by specific department titles. For example, in some corporations the tax department is considered a part of the law department, while in others it is classified as a financial operation. Thus, using the function approach in your job search will help insure that interesting positions are not foreclosed simply because the particular department designation used by the organization does not match the one you specify.

Taxes

Considering the total activity of a corporate tax department, it is not hard to understand that there is a perennial debate as to whether this is a financial or legal function. At the entry level, much of the work is involved in the preparation of the more than 500 tax returns that must be filed to meet federal, state, and local tax requirements. In addition, reports are prepared for tax returns on income, sales, use, property, capital stock franchises, payroll, license fees, etc., and records are kept of all these returns and reports for reference. In large corporations, the amounts involved can easily be $100,000,000 or more.

Tax departments, however, are involved in a great many more activities. In more senior positions, the duties are likely to include one or more of the following:

> Supervising the review of the tax returns of domestic affiliates and foreign affiliates if the company has them. Supervising the conduct of federal, state, and local (and possibly foreign) tax audits and examinations and developing an amicable professional relationship with the federal income tax auditors and state and local tax officials.

> Supervising and reviewing preparation and argument of protests of administrative actions and claims for refund, and participating in court litigation either directly or through review of activities of outside counsel.

Advising management with respect to the tax effects of completed transactions and suggesting possible alternatives. Frequently there is a good deal of work in relation to real estate and personal property taxes.

Seeking to lawfully influence proposed tax legislation and regulation by meeting with members of the Congressional tax writing committees and their staff, as well as with members of the U.S. Treasury Department, either individually or through various trade associations and other professional groups. Similar activities will be undertaken with state and local officials.

Conducting seminars, meetings, and the like to inform appropriate corporate personnel of relevant developments in the tax field affecting their operations.

Advising the international division of a multinational corporation regarding taxes of foreign countries and the related effects of foreign operations on United States taxes to determine proper planning and compliance.

Initiating tax advice as part of the corporation's financial planning process.

In view of the responsibilities involved and the nature of the functions performed, some corporations will require that all persons in the tax department be lawyers, while others will list this as a desirable qualification. Most corporations, however, will insist on an undergraduate degree in accounting with special value placed on advanced degrees relating to tax work.

Employee Relations

Depending upon the corporation, you may also find this activity entitled *industrial relations, labor relations,* or *personnel administration.* To add to the confusion, you will find that no matter how it is designated, this area of the corporation's activities covers several distinct functions, each of which will be discussed separately. The desirability of having legally trained persons employed in these activities is evident in the substantial number of lawyers now occupying these posts.

Most companies appear to apply the designation *labor relations* specifically to the activities surrounding the development and imple-

mentation of company labor policies and procedures and its relationships with unions. Individuals working in this area may be involved
in one or more areas of concern. This work may include negotiation
of the various corporate labor agreements within previously approved
economic limits, as well as monitoring labor relations matters
throughout the corporation to insure adherence to applicable labor
agreements and corporate labor relations policies.

In some instances, persons in this field will develop and present the
company's position in arbitration cases, or handle National Labor Relations Board (NLRB) unfair labor practice charges and representation
situations. On a continuing basis, they will review labor relations
policies and practices and labor agreements to insure compliance with
applicable federal and state laws.

Persons in this field will find it imperative to keep current on proposed labor legislation, National Labor Relations Board (NLRB) decisions, court decisions and Equal Employment Opportunity Commission (EEO) rulings, including safety, security, and fair employment
practices, to determine what effect, if any, these developments will
have on corporate labor agreements, practices, policies, and procedures, and to see that all company personnel are kept informed. Upon
occasion, they may participate in the settlement of labor disputes, ar-
bitrations, grievances, and other employee and union relations matters.

Persons in this field may work to maintain effective rapport with
local union representatives and will often cooperate with those in wage
and salary administration and with other industry representatives,
either directly or through trade associations, to insure harmonious
employee relation through maintenance of equitable and competitive
wage policies.

Still another area within the employee relations field is that of
employee benefits. This area can involve the planning, development,
implementation, and administration of a variety of benefit programs,
including, but not limited to, medical and dental insurance, long-term
disability, retirement benefits, and may involve the financing of such
programs. Such work can also encompass dealing with estates, ir-
revocable trusts, and similar matters. An important and integral part
of this program is the communication regarding employee benefits
directly to the employees involved.

A relative newcomer in the employee relations area is the person
working in the equal employment opportunities program. Such work
involves the development of policies to insure compliance with equal

employment opportunity legislation, the analysis of company practices for compliance, and the proposal of recommended courses of action. In most corporations, this activity appears as separate from the labor relations function, but obviously it must be closely coordinated with that operation.

You will also find persons with legal training working in the administration of workers' compensation programs, in the recruitment and training of employees, and in wage and salary administration.

Financial

No corporation could long exist without a financial control center, which may be known variously as the *treasurer's office, comptroller's office,* or the *accounting and finance department.* In some corporations it also includes a separate and distinct internal audit department which on a day-to-day basis performs duties similar to those of an outside auditor but in greater depth.

The functions of the financial office may vary somewhat according to the nature of the corporation's business activities. Its activities will probably include the establishment and maintenance of companywide accounting and reporting policies and practices. These must be compatible with all applicable rules and regulations as well as meet the company's financial goal. If there is an internal audit department, the financial office will work with it to assure compliance.

The financial office will also develop and maintain a financial reporting and analysis system, which permits management to develop both short-range and long-range planning. In addition, financial statements and reports must be prepared for investors, lenders, the Securities and Exchange Commission (SEC), the board of directors, financial analysts, and investment bankers.

This office must also analyze the potential effect on the company's financial statements resulting from proposed equity changes, regulatory actions, changes in world financial conditions, and changes in accounting practices. It is responsible for the receipt, disbursement, banking, and protection and custody of funds, securities, and financial instruments. The office evaluates the need for procurement of funds and investment of surplus. In some instances the financial office will also be responsible for customer credit arrangements and the negotiation of term loan agreements. Budget preparation and monitoring and financial forecasting are also major responsibilities.

Because of the financial officer's day-to-day involvement in every aspect of the company's activity, it is not surprising that so many of the presidents of corporations should be drawn from their ranks. Many of these are lawyers as well. Keep in mind, however, that many organizations will require an MBA degree in addition to legal training for employment in the financial area.

Opportunities in the financial area are not confined solely to industry. Opportunities can be found in the nation's banking and financial institutions, investment houses, and brokerage firms.

Perhaps you are already aware that increasing numbers of trust officers in banks are legally trained persons. However, the ranks of commercial-loan officers, mortgage officers, loan counselors, and foreign-exchange traders also include legally trained persons.

Banks, insurance companies, and brokerage and investment houses often employ the services of financial analysts, some of whom are aided in their work by a legal background. These individuals analyze and interpret data concerning investments, price, yield, stability, and future trends, drawing their information from daily stock and bond reports, financial periodicals, securities manuals, and personal interviews. They summarize data setting forth current and long-term trends in investment risks and measurable economic influences pertinent to the status of investments. In some instances, they may transmit buy-and-sell orders to brokers based on their analysis.

Keep in mind that every financial institution also has its own internal financial controls office with functions similar to those of its counterparts in industry.

Real Estate

The three categories of nonlegal work in business and industry just described, now frequently performed by legally trained persons, may vary somewhat from corporation to corporation, but the same basic operation will be common to all. In the real estate area, however, functions may vary widely according to the nature of the company's business. Detailed descriptions of all the various activities that might be performed would result in a volume several times the size of this one. Rather, a review of some of the more common aspects of this activity should set your imagination working regarding other interesting possibilities.

Petroleum and gas producers, wood products and paper producers, and all types of mining operations are examples of types of industries that rely on control through lease or purchase of substantial tracts of real estate to produce the natural resources upon which the industry is based. Once a company has decided on the parcels it wishes to acquire, individuals, usually lawyers, are sent out to directly negotiate with property owners for the purchase or leasing of the property. These positions, called variously land representatives, lease agents, or by similar titles, are often entry level positions.

These individuals negotiate and renegotiate such agreements as leases, options, and realty contracts covering such activities as exploration, drilling, and producing activities and work out royalty payments with the landowners. Obviously, as the holdings desired increase in size and value, senior members of the real estate office with in-depth experience in this work will also be involved.

One of the important functions of a real estate department involves condemnations and other public takings in which the department will be involved in negotiations with public officials and working with the law department and outside counsel.

Backing up this activity will be a leasing department which directs the entire operation, including studying the leases bought and prices paid, as well as negotiating with competing companies in order to determine the expenditure necessary to obtain leases and other contracts in the desired areas. Final decisions will be made on all agreements and contracts for purchase, sale, and acquisition of land leases in mineral and royalty rights, as well as the determination and specifics of the date of termination of lease rentals.

Following up on this activity will be the department that supervises the payments on and fulfillment of terms of leases and contracts, the maintenance of files and records, and the preparation of reports on such subjects as lease expiration dates, disposition of lease purchases, and rentals due. Making sure of a clear title may be required in any of these areas. Somewhat similar activities must also be undertaken by pipeline companies and utilities in bringing their products to market.

In addition, the business concerns just mentioned, as well as almost every other industry, have real estate people who are responsible for the administration of corporate and divisional land usage. This work can involve the acquisition of sites for new buildings, purchasing land parcels adjacent to plants, community protection, disposing of surplus land, and arranging for short- and long-term leases. This activity may even include the accumulation of data involved in site selection. During construction, securing right-of-way for utility lines and pipe lines may be necessary. The roads, bridges, and utility systems that must be maintained during that time will have to be determined and negotiations undertaken for access routes and restoration of roads and surfaces.

In all these areas the skills developed in law school of analyzing and assembling facts are highly utilized. Furthermore, a better than average aptitude for negotiation is important in real estate activities.

For corporations with substantial real estate activity, it is not uncommon for senior members of the department to be required to be lawyers in order that they may undertake the drafting of leases and contracts, lease amendments and modification agreements, and subleases. Often they may be required to furnish opinions regarding what legal steps, if any, are to be taken on such matters as zoning, variations from restrictions imposed by various governmental authorities, law suits, and other matters. They may also be involved in hearings before planning boards, city and town councils, zoning boards, and boards of appeals to obtain approvals for various matters requiring special handling. Corporations with lesser activity in the real estate area usually find that this activity can comfortably be handled within the legal department.

Merchandising concerns and those industries that market their products directly to the public, as well as franchising organizations, may be involved in the purchase or leasing of shopping center facilities or retail outlets and the disposal of obsolete or unprofitable units.

In some industries with extensive dealerships, buy-outs and takeovers of dealer property is a specialized activity which involves agreements to sell and purchase, leases, sale contracts, releases, stock certificates, exchanges, inventory agreements, and settlements. Because of the individuality of these arrangements, most of the documents must be specially prepared and tailored to cover the particular situation.

One corporate activity that is extremely difficult to classify is the responsibility for the insurance of its real property assets against loss and damage. Classification is less important, however, than the company's very real need to develop, monitor, and maintain the appropriate and vital coverage.

Banks and other financial institutions are involved in loan programs covering everything from modest single family dwellings to huge real estate development projects. Some financial institutions and insurance companies are heavily involved in real-estate investment programs.

Independent real-estate development projects may be of substantial size. These projects not only involve the original development but may involve sales and leasing for occupancy. The nature of the work in all of these areas is such that lawyer skills are increasingly proving to be advantageous to effective job performance.

An important function which those with legal training can play in banks and other financial institutions is the reading, analysis, commenting on, and assisting in the observance of a myriad of federal and state rules and regulations. Usually the responsibility for keeping track of such rules and regulations is assigned to those with legal training, who may also have responsibility for seeing that the rules and regulations are understood and adhered to.

The number of attorneys employed by any given organization will depend on the type and degree of involvement in real estate matters which the company has. For example, there are hundreds of attorneys working for title insurance companies, which use them in all phases of their operation including title examinations and issuance of policies. In contrast, there are only a few lawyers who have found employment handling the real estate news in newspapers, magazines, and business publications.

Government Relations/Public Affairs/Consumer Affairs/Public Relations

Although markedly different in function, all of the areas covered in this section have one thing in common — they seek a positive outreach and impact by the company upon the public and government.

Many areas of corporate activity are closely related to meeting the requirements of various laws and the regulations issued by governmental agencies and departments. In the government relations area, also, the industry seeks to bring its influence to bear upon pending legislation. It does so in several different ways.

The first step is a continuing analysis of all pending legislation, whether federal, state, or local, for its possible impact on the company's operation. When it is determined that particular legislation under consideration would relate to the company's interests, the second step is to define the position of the company. This determination is made in consultation with officials of the company, interested departments, and in many instances with trade association boards and committees. The position taken may be for or against the proposed legislation, or may simply be concerned with recommending changes or amendments.

The third step is presenting the company's view to the appropriate government officials. This presentation may involve formal written or verbal statements, or simply informal discussions. The latter meetings are facilated by maintaining a cordial relationship with government officials most likely to be concerned with the matters under consideration. Development of these relationships is a major responsibility of the government relations personnel, but they also cooperate with other departments having direct relationships with specific agencies, as, for example, might be the case with the employee relations group and the office of the EEOC.

When pending legislation is of industrywide concern, the company's views may be coordinated through professional or trade associations. In fact, trade associations also offer employment opportunities for those interested in government relations because they frequently represent companies which are not sufficiently large to maintain an internal government relations staff.

From time to time, matters may develop that go far beyond specific company or industry concerns, and the need arises to develop public opinion for or against proposed legislation and regulation or both. One such example is the area of energy-related legislation. In addition to coordinating the activities of various company departments that may be involved with the issue, there will also be efforts to coordinate with the work being done by industry, consumer groups, and others who may have interests in the matter.

In the consumer affairs area, individuals are working to assure that consumer complaints and information requests are promptly and fairly handled and that the buyer has accurate and useful product and warranty information. In addition, consumer affairs persons may also provide guidance and advice in terms of product safety and in doing so will undoubtedly be working with a broad segment of the company's programs ranging from its contacts with vendors to engineering administration. Close coordination with the legal department is essential in handling inquiries from concerned organizations and government agencies and in an exchange of information that will assure a thorough understanding of the legal impact of government policy affecting product safety and consumer affairs.

The environmental concerns of some companies, aside from regulatory compliance, have led to the development of activities relating the company's position to concerned individuals and organizations. In general, the activities in this area will be similar to those pursued in consumer affairs and product safety.

Upon occasion, all of these activities may be grouped under a single designation such as public relations or public affairs. In others, the public relations function will primarily relate to providing information to the business community and those individuals interested in the company's business concerning the company, its products, its officers, and its plans and programs.

Creating and projecting a company's image and position in response to the broad interests and concerns of the public and its government is a day-to-day concern of business organizations and involves increasing numbers of persons in these activities. More and more legally trained persons are finding that their particular skills can make a substantial contribution to these efforts.

Traffic

The type of activities which go under the heading *traffic* will vary considerably depending upon the nature of the corporation. If a company's activities involve the movement of raw materials to production areas and finished products to consumers, warehouses, and other storage locations, then plans and procedures for their transportation must be formulated and monitored. In some cases, this process involves the ownership or leasing of private carriers.

If you have never been close to corporate life, it is highly unlikely that you have previously considered traffic activities as an area in which your legal training could be used to advantage, yet there are numbers of persons like you who are doing just that.

Individuals involved in this area must analyze the transportation facilities and commodity classifications to determine the most efficient and economical shipping rates and routes, and must furnish such data to other departments and customers. Investigations of damages during shipment, delays, overcharges, and insurance charges must be initiated. In some instances, duties of such persons may also include studies in product planning, warehousing, packaging, and loading to reduce shipping costs. This area may involve planning and purchase of transportation equipment or the leasing of such equipment and of warehouse facilities from other concerns. These activities may involve appearances before the Interstate Commerce Commission (ICC) and other federal and state agencies on tariffs and similar matters of interest to private carriers.

Persons working in traffic with transportation companies involving the movement of people as well as freight, by air, motor, rail, and water have similar activities together with additional responsibilities. They must formulate and determine freight or passenger classifications and applicable rates according to company policies and governmental regulations. Such persons are constantly evaluating existing rate structures to determine their economic suitability and the schedules to determine adequacy of service.

New rate tables and schedules may be developed to meet changing company economic needs and expansion or line abandonment plans or both. All proposed rates and schedules must be filed with regulatory agencies, and testimony at hearings by the regulatory agencies may be required for both proposed and existing rates and schedules.

Contracts must be negotiated with other companies for the transportation of freight or passengers in areas not served by the company, including the determination of the division of interline revenue. Supervision of or coordination with receiving and shipping departments, reservation and ticket offices, and those engaged in soliciting freight or passenger business will also be important functions.

In radio and television broadcasting, the traffic department arranges for the leasing of wire facilities to transmit radio and television programs to the individual stations of a network. In addition, contact must be made with communication companies to arrange for facilities to transmit programs from the point of broadcast origin to network stations. Affiliated stations must be informed of charges to be made for commercial broadcasts and for those programs requiring special facility hookups in addition to the availability of noncommercial programs available for broadcast.

Possibly because lawyers outside of corporate activity have been unaware of the existence of these programs necessary to so many corporations, only a relatively few lawyers are presently working in this area. It is, however, by its very nature, an activity in which legal training would prove advantageous to job performance. The work involves much data collection, analysis of facts, recommendation of action based on that analysis, negotiation, and working with regulatory agencies. How better to use a law school education?

Insurance

It would be hard to imagine any corporation or business organization without an insurance program, or risk management as it is sometimes known. The only differences are essentially those dictated by the varying needs of the organization and the number of persons necessary to accomplish the individual company's objectives.

Several distinct activities are involved.

(1) It is essential to recognize *all* corporate risks of accidental occurrences, both actual and potential, in the areas of property, loss of income, workers' compensation, and liability. Determining such risks may involve surveys of company property, assets, and operations to classify hazards and evaluate insurable risks. Consultation with engineering, personnel, and financial departments may be necessary to plan insurance risk coverage as well as negotiation with insurance brokers to purchase adequate coverage at the lowest possible cost.

(2) It will be necessary for a person working in this area to keep up with insurance industry developments, such as new areas of coverage that may be planned, as well as current insurance legislation in order that risk coverage may be changed or modified as needed.

(3) Records and reports must be prepared on experience-cost-analysis and safety and loss prevention summaries for the guidance of management.

(4) Negotiation of the settlement of loss claims with insurance carriers and cooperation with the legal department to provide information for the litigation of insured risks will be among the responsibilities in this area. In addition, all insurance contracts will need constant auditing to determine any changes in insurance requirements and coverage needed.

Within the insurance industry itself, there are legally trained persons working in almost every aspect of the company's activities. These will include most of the common areas of concern to all corporate entities, as well as the development or revision of specific insurance programs to meet anticipated demand.

Those areas of insurance company activity comparable to those found in other industries need not be reiterated. Entry into these positions will, in most cases, be comparable to that in other industries.

Many insurance companies utilize a special entry level position to thoroughly acquaint new additions to their staff with the special problems, procedures, and policies peculiar to the insurance industry, and to the specific company. That position is commonly known as *claims adjustor.*

This individual investigates claims for loss and damage filed in conjunction with a specific insurance policy and tries to effect out-of-court settlement. He or she will examine the claim form and other records to determine insurance coverage, interview or correspond with the claimant and witnesses, consult police and hospital records, and inspect property damage to determine the extent of the company's liability, varying the method of investigation according to the type of insurance.

A report of the findings will be prepared and an effort to negotiate settlement will be made with the claimant. When a settlement cannot be negotiated, the claims adjustor will make a recommendation for litigation to the legal department. Although he or she will not be directly involved in the litigation, the claims adjustor may attend the litigation hearings. The claims adjustor does not settle life or accident-and-sickness claims. The individual's title may be designated, however, according to the type of claim with which he or she is dealing such as casualty insurance, fidelity and surety bonds, fire insurance, or marine insurance.

These positions not only give day-to-day experience with the practical implementation of the company's insurance programs, but they provide a unique opportunity to observe first-hand the various opportunities for advancement to positions peculiar to industry operations.

One such position is that of underwriter, whose duties include review of applications for insurance to evaluate the degree of risk involved and to accept those that follow the company's underwriting policies. Company records will be reviewed to determine the amount of insurance in force on a single risk or group of closely related risks, as well as evaluating the possibility of losses due to catastrophe or excessive insurance. Risks which are too excessive to obligate the company will be declined or reinsurance may be authorized. If the risk is substandard, the underwriter may limit the company's obligation by decreasing the value of the policy, specifying applicable endorsements, or apply a rating to insure safe and profitable distribution of risks. Underwriters will usually work in only a single area such as accident-and-sickness, automobile, bond, fire, liability, life, marine, property, and special risks.

Legally trained persons are also to be found frequently in the local and district offices of insurance companies. Often they will start in sales positions where the opportunity is provided to become familiar with the potential insurance needs of the clients. Legal training has proved helpful in allowing the individual to explain most effectively how the coverage suggested will specifically answer the client's needs. Legally trained persons are also utilized in selecting and writing endorsements and riders, reviewing policies to be sure that the coverage is as contemplated, and, perhaps even more importantly, participating in the handling of insurance claims.

Regulatory Compliance

In a proliferation of government regulatory activity at all levels — federal, state, and local — hardly a business or industry remains untouched by the need to assure compliance with the various rules and regulations. Often the economic well-being of the company will be at stake.

Because of the complexities involved in assuring compliance and the importance of this function to the economic aspects of a company, it is not surprising to find more and more legally trained persons gravitating to this area. In some companies compliance is handled directly by the operating unit affected by the regulation, such as equal employment opportunity assigned to the employee relations department, but in other companies all regulatory compliance matters are supervised from a central unit.

It would be impossible to list here all of the types of activities which may be carried on under the general designation of regulatory compliance. However, a partial listing of the functions performed in a single company involved in the production of drugs, cosmetics, and devices in meeting the requirements of the Food and Drug Administration (FDA), the U.S. Department of Agriculture (USDA), and the Federal Trade Commission (FTC) concerned with these areas of production will give you some idea of the nature of the work:

> Coordinates and supervises all the activities involved in the preparation of technical data for submission to government agencies such as the FDA, USDA, and FTC.
> Gathers, organizes, prepares, assembles, and submits information for investigational new drug submissions and new drug ap-

plications in accordance with new drug regulations, reviewing them for completeness and accuracy.

Negotiates with the FDA with regard to product claims, and coordinates contacts for the company with FDA scientific review personnel.

Serves as the company representative during plant inspections by FDA personnel.

Coordinates training sessions for manufacturing and control personnel under simulated FDA inspection conditions.

Reviews and approves labeling, advertising, and specifications to assure compliance with FDA regulations.

Coordinates the preparation and submits periodic reports including literature surveys required by government agencies when marketing new drugs.

Assembles and summarizes data in response to specific trade association or government agency requests for data.

Acts as liaison in coordinating activities between the company and government agencies by acquiring information on new guidelines, regulations, and amendments.

Summarizes regulatory information to be supplied to other operating units and companies.

Obviously, working in the above outlined area would require a technical background even though legal training would provide substantial assistance in determining the requirements to be met. Not all regulatory compliance areas, however, will have this technical requirement, although familiarity with the operational aspects of the functions being regulated would be essential to monitor compliance. Thus the individual working in traffic would need to know and understand the rates and schedules used by the company to assure that ICC regulations were being met.

Another area of activity is that of the collection, reading, commenting on, analyzing, preparing summaries of, and training others in compliance with, governmental regulations. Legal training is useful also and frequently employed in the formulation of plans and procedures for compliance. Lawyers are apt better to understand regulations than laymen and to determine whether contemplated procedures will accomplish necessary results.

Corporate Secretarial

Long before legally trained persons were working in the regulatory compliance area, lawyers were involved in the corporate secretarial area. Indeed, it is not uncommon that the title "Secretary" is also held by the General Counsel. Thus, this area was one of the first to demonstrate that nonlegal positions within a corporation could benefit from the attention of legally trained minds.

The corporate secretarial office is responsible for keeping the minutes of the proceedings of meetings of shareholders, board of directors, and sometimes the executive committee. It maintains records containing specified information regarding the shareholders, notifies them of meetings, and furnishes proxy ballots when required and in accordance with SEC rules. An important function is the preparation of proxy statements.

The secretary is responsible for the corporate seal and is responsible for having it affixed to documents as directed by the board of directors. The board may also direct the keeping of such other records as it deems appropriate.

The secretary, and usually assistant secretaries as well, are elected by the board of directors, but other members of the staff may not be.

Purchasing and Contract Administration

It may seem a little odd to join in a single category purchasing, which is concerned with the assembling of supplies, equipment, and services essential to the company's production, and contract administration, which is concerned essentially with the sale of products. Yet in reality they are closely related inasmuch as both are primarily concerned with the developing and monitoring of contracts.

One of the important roles which lawyers can and do play in the purchasing and sales areas relates to the "battle of the fine print," i.e., the difficulties that all buyers and sellers have with the differences between the terms and conditions of purchase orders and of terms of sales. The working out of these differences, and in many instances the development of basic agreements between purchasers and sellers becomes a function in which legal training plays an important role. Likewise the development of an understanding on the part of both management and buyers and salesmen of the effects of differences in the fine print can frequently be left to those with legal training in purchasing and sales departments.

In the purchasing area responsibilities may encompass a variety of activities. As the sums involved may run in the millions of dollars during the year, it is probable that in most instances, bids will be sought from suppliers based on the specifications of one or more departments within the company. Frequently it may be necessary to survey vendors' plants or facilities to assess such factors as production capacity, quality control, and financial status to determine the vendors' ability to meet the specifications.

When the supply contract has been completed, the purchasing area will monitor conformance to delivery and cost schedules. If technical problems arise, the purchasing function will serve as the coordinating unit between the vendor and the various company departments involved in the purchase.

Contract administration is closely allied to the sales and marketing functions. In some companies, the work is also split into commercial and government areas. Its essential function, however, remains the same: monitoring the execution of the company's contracts as to price, performance, and schedules.

Accomplishing this goal requires coordination with purchasing, production, quality assurance, and engineering functions. Records and reports may need to be prepared for customers, and contract modifications may have to be negotiated. This area of responsibility alone can be tremendously complex. Consider, for example, the complexities involved in the monitoring of a single contract for the development of an experimental aircraft for the Department of Defense.

In addition, this area may also be responsible for the gathering of data for bid proposals and may analyze all major bids to determine why the company was not awarded the contract, as well as recommending procedures to be used in obtaining future contract awards.

Such data can be of profound assistance to the marketing function. Close coordination with the financial and credit areas is also most essential.

Marketing

This area is the cornerstone upon which the company bases its whole existence. Without the sale of its products or services, the very reason for the existence of the company, profits, disappears.

The marketing strategy used will vary widely depending upon whether the customer is individual, corporate, or governmental, upon the cost of the product or service, and even upon such factors as geography. Nevertheless, all marketing involves several basic functions.

The first of these is analzying the market. Who are the customers for the company's products or services? Are there other consumers, not yet identified, for whom the company's products or services might be useful or desirable? What are the customer's specific needs and how do the company's products or services meet that need? Answers to these and related questions must be found.

The next step is to decide upon the best approach or approaches to both the present and the potential market. This process may involve a study of competitor strategies, keeping aware of new developments within one's own company that may be of interest to the customer, developing a media advertising program, and keeping close contacts with key personnel in the offices of potential customers.

The third and final step is the developing and monitoring of staff support for the strategy or strategies decided upon. This activity may involve employing an advertising agency and development of a field sales force and sales training programs.

Until very recently, only a handful of lawyers had chosen to work in the marketing area, possibly because of an oversimplified idea of the responsibilities involved. Now, however, many companies are eagerly seeking legally trained persons in an effort to avoid antitrust or regulatory compliance problems. One recent illustration may serve to indicate the reasons for this new attitude.

An advertising agency contracted with a federal government department to produce some films, a type of account they had not had before. Industry custom and union contracts dictated that those involved in the filming would be flown to the site first class. The government contract, however, specified that first-class air travel was permitted only in highly exceptional circumstances. The conflict was not noted and upon the completion of the assignment, the advertising agency billed the government department in line with its customary commercial account practice. It took more than a year to get the matter straightened out. A legally trained account executive might well have been expected to be alert to a potential conflict, such as this, so that the problem could have been cleared up before it developed.

Security

If the word "security" conjures up a picture of a lone guard at a plant gate, you are undoubtedly wondering why this category has been included in material on nonlegal positions for legally trained persons. Actually, the plant guard is only one visible evidence of the vast area of responsibility of the security department, which must develop and monitor a program that will prevent the loss of company property and equipment from theft.

Far less visible but certainly essential today is the protection of company documents and data, and this problem in recent years has become increasingly complex. Thus, current concerns include protection against computer data theft by unauthorized persons with sufficient technical knowledge to tie themselves into the company's system, and the possibility of massive credit card counterfeiting. Prevention of industrial espionage has become a major area of corporate concern in recent years.

If the company is involved in the manufacture of products or the processing of material or data for the federal government, compliance with the federal security regulations must also be planned and monitored. Consultation with government officials may be necessary to obtain interpretations of these rules, and requests for deviations may be necessary where undue hardship is involved.

Implementation of security procedures in the long run will be no better than their implementation by the personnel involved or working directly with sensitive areas. Thus, manuals must be produced and training sessions held to inform personnel of their duties and responsibilities. Frequent rechecks are necessary to insure that laxness in procedures does not occur due to a passage of time without incident.

A lawyer who is staff assistant to the head of the security department of a large insurance company, for instance, in the performance of his or her duties needs to know how to investigate security problems, how to detect crimes, how to deal with customers and employees suspected of irregularities without getting the company involved in false arrests or litigation, and how to assist police, the FBI and district and United States attorneys in the handling of investigations and prosecutions. In this position he or she may have to know as much criminal law as a good prosecutor.

As business and industry grow ever more complex, so do their protection needs. Legally trained persons working in this area are sure to find new challenges to their skills and inventiveness with every passing year.

Potpourri

The areas discussed are those in which most legally trained persons are currently filling nonlegal positions. Anyone contemplating a business management career, however, should be aware that the foregoing is far from a complete spectrum of the possibilities. An active imagination can easily expand the number of opportunities. Just a few examples of positions currently filled by lawyers to get you started:

Administrating subsidiary rights for a book publisher includes promotion of forthcoming and backlisted publications to book clubs, magazines, reprint houses, and motion picture studios and the appropriate followup. When interest in purchase is developed, these administrators negotiate deals with organizations for the sale of specific items.

The export function for any company with foreign sales and service outlets. The work involves negotiation of contracts with foreign sales and distribution centers to establish outlets, conversion of products from U.S. to foreign standards as well as the handling of shipping details, including export licenses, customs declarations, and packing, shipping, and routing of the products. In addition, persons working in this area may be involved in the preparation of foreign-language sales manuals and maintaining current information on import-export tariffs, licenses, and restrictions. A word of caution comes from the recruiting and employment manager of one corporation with extensive overseas business: "In the past we have received a number of inquiries from individuals possessing a legal background and desiring employment relating to international marketing opportunities. Unfortunately, most positions that become available in the international business area are filled by individuals from foreign countries having a varied degree of practical experience."

Industrial development for a railroad. Such work involves negotiations with representatives of business and industrial organizations and community leaders to stimulate industrial development within the territory served by the railroad. Information on such things as available plant sites, availability and quality of water resources, tax rates in given communities, and the proportion of the total work force having specified skills must be gathered, sometimes in cooperation with representatives of state governments, public utilities, universities, and similar groups. Negotiations must be carrried on with communities, state governments, public utilities, universities, and similar groups. Negotiation with representatives of communities, businesses, and public utilities representatives along the railroad line must be undertaken to eliminate obstacles to industrial development and to development of harmonious relations between local citizens and new plants.

Merchandise control for a retail organization with a substantial number of outlets. In this area records are kept on all merchandise on hand and data on sales on all items of merchandise in the various branch stores. Those working in this area are responsible for seeing that merchandise from the general stock is delivered to the branch stores or moved from one branch to another as sales may require. They provide information to buyers to assist in making decisions on the need for current or future buying activity.

In assessing the variety of possibilities, also keep in mind that almost every business and each industry has unique functions peculiar to it alone. Consider the operational differences between hotels, retailers, banks, mining operations, and producers of heavy industrial equipment. As you analyze the functions involved in any operation, imagine how you might use your legal training to enhance your job performance within those functions.

3

What Are the Possibilities with the Associations and other Organizations?

There are a number of new and expanding possibilities in the utilization of legally trained persons by organizations that might not have considered them only a few years ago. The reason for this development is quite simple. Such persons offer special training and understanding which these organizations can utilize. Frequently law graduates are hired by employers on the basis of other qualifications. Only later the employer realizes the value that legal training has in performing many other duties. Once one lawyer is hired, many organizations continue to seek others, sometimes to the exclusion of nonlawyers who held the positions previously. Among those types of organizations that have hired increasing numbers of legally trained persons are the following.

Associations

Bar associations, other professional and occupation-related associations, trade associations, sports associations, and hobby associations range in scope from the American Bar Association to the National Football League. All, however, are organizations that undertake to provide benefits to members, whether these be individuals or organizations or both.

The services provided to members will include such matters as administrative management of the organization and dissemination of particular information relating to the special interests of the group. They may also include such diverse activities as fund-raising, legislative review, lobbying, planning of meetings, contract negotiation, and developing educational seminars and membership promotion.

While organizational structures vary widely depending upon the size of the association and the nature of its needed activities, the work holds particular appeal for lawyers since their legal skills are often directly applicable and it is possible that individual interests and hobbies of the lawyers are represented by the particular organization.

Do not let the term "association" as applied to these organizations confuse you. Many are identified by such terms as "league," "society," "fraternity," "alliance" or "institute." All are essentially the same, for they have been formed to further the interests of members, be they individuals or groups. The staff serves essentially as a secretariat for the organization and can vary in number from one person to hundreds. Staff size will determine the nature of the particular opportunity, be it the Jack-of-all-trades of the one-person staff or the specialized role required when many are employed.

National Service Organizations

This category includes such organizations as Kiwanis, Rotary, United Way, League of Women Voters, Boy Scouts of America, Girl Scouts of America, and the Sierra Club.

The organizational setup of these bodies is different from the association in that their constituency is made up of local clubs or groups, which are primarily involved in service activities to the community in which they are located. The central office serves to coordinate individual groups and provide them with educational, promotional, fund-raising, and other support activities in addition to the general administrative functions necessary to the health and well-being of any organization.

International Service Organizations

Included in this group are such organizations as the Red Cross, the Organization of American States, and the United Nations, including the specialized agencies of the latter such as the International Monetary Fund (IMF), the United Nations Educational, Scientific and Cultural Organization (UNESCO), and the World Health Organization (WHO).

It is difficult to distinguish these groups from the national service organizations in many respects except to note that their activities maintain an international basis of service. In these groups the structure frequently varies far more widely than is true of the national service organizations. Nevertheless, the administrative function remains very much the same. It is in the realm of the service activities that the great variety arises, with the differences depending upon the nature of the particular organization. Because most of these organizations are engaged in providing assistance to the needy around the world, fund-raising is usually a major activity.

If this is an area of interest to you, you should take a second look at the national service organizations. The division is rather arbitrary and many of the organizations that are primarily on a national level such as the Red Cross do have, however, extensive international programs. If you look only for the designation "international," you may overlook many interesting possibilities.

Publishers

By the end of law school, most students are at least aware of the existence of legal publishers even though the tasks that lawyers perform within these organizations may be unclear. There are, as usual, a variety of administrative opportunities as well as the editorial functions for which legal training is virtually a prerequisite. On the other hand, very few students are aware of the many opportunities that exist throughout the general publishing world.

Every hardcover book, paperback, magazine, newspaper has a publisher. In addition, there are publishers on virtually every conceivable subject for schoolbooks, encyclopedias, specialty books, and periodicals. Each of these publishers employs editorial staff who usually have a specialized background in the particular subject peculiar to the publication. There are also those involved in the administration of the total enterprise, as well as individuals involved in specialized activities that are peculiar to the publishing world. They are involved in such tasks as negotiating paperback rights for hardcover books, movie rights, distribution arrangements, serialization rights, and the releasing of trademark rights for consumer products. If you have been thinking about publishing only in editorial terms, you have been missing a fascinating group of career possibilities.

Educational Institutions

Educational institutions are increasingly utilizing legally trained persons for teaching positions at all levels. Some of the areas where this development has been most noticeable are:

Acquainting the general public with the concept and operation of our legal system.

Educating law enforcement officers in the proper application of laws.

Teaching law-related business courses to business students.

Educating practicing professionals about legal applications of their work.

While special teaching credentials may be required for some of these posts, legal training itself is an essential component of the qualifications for the job.

Educational institutions also offer a variety of administrative positions with educational institutions. Not only must there be persons to manage and direct these organizations, but there is often the need for fund-raising and closely related activities.

Health Care Institutions

Concern with rising health care costs has brought a new dimension to the administrative functions of health care institutions. Cost containment is a complicated matter that brings many legal as well as administrative problems into play. With them come new challenges for lawyers, presenting a dramatic example of how new opportunities for lawyers are created by economic and social forces beyond traditional concerns. Health care institutions are not alone in being subject to these developments. Every career-minded person should be aware of these throughout his productive years.

Of course, these new developments do not diminish the need for the management and administrative functions that have been a traditional need in these organizations. They also share a need with educational institutions for fund-raising activities. Any medical training or experience related to it would obviously heighten consideration for a person in any of these posts, but legal training is also proving invaluable in the smooth functioning of these operations.

Media Organizations

The expanding world of media is no longer limited to newspapers, magazines, books, radio and television. Today electronic publishing, cable television, pay television, and international data communications are rapidly becoming household words. With technological advances have come the need for people who understand the legal implications of their application. One such example is the need for negotiators in the purchase of movies for cable television even before they are released in theaters, as well as the determination of what information can be legally exported from the country by means of satellite and what restrictions exist in its transmission across the borders of several countries. The persons who provide these services to their organizations have proven their work is essential. Since technological advances in this area have not yet reached a plateau, inevitably there will be more and exciting new possibilities for legally trained persons in the future.

Management Consulting Firms

Management consulting firms have existed for 30 years or more. Originally their staffs were composed almost entirely of business school graduates and engineers. Many such firms have found, however, that including legally trained persons on their staffs increase the capacity of the organization to provide services to their clients. The primary activity of these groups is to advise businesses on more efficient and profitable methods of organization, production, and management.

Some management consultant firms devote their entire attention to the task of management recruitment. In some cases the consulting firms devote the attention of a particular department to this activity. Their recruiting efforts are usually confined to management positions because the substantial fees which are charged to the employer for their services make these uneconomic for lower-level positions.

In recent years a specialized type of recruitment service has developed devoted solely to the locating of lawyer applicants for available legal opportunities. Few, if any, will accept law graduate applicants, requiring that the lawyers have at least a few years experience. One major factor in this limitation is the organized student placement programs that are now in operation.

Having someone who can understand the legal ramifications of the changes being recommended and who can evaluate candidates who offer credentials in the legal field has made the legally trained person a valuable addition to the staff. It is rare now to find a management consulting firm of any size that does not include lawyers on its staff.

Accounting Firms

Once almost exclusively comprised of accounting and business school graduates, accounting firms are increasingly finding that individuals with this specialized background who also have legal training expand the depth and quality of their services. Some of the biggest of these firms have recently added law-office management consulting departments. While accounting and management procedures apply equally to law offices and to business organizations, nevertheless there are differences, and the management of those differences can be of utmost importance to the individual law office.

In addition to the auditing work which these organizations routinely perform, they have undertaken a great deal of tax planning work, and this area has attracted substantial numbers of lawyers because of the legal implications involved. Most of these firms will insist upon an accounting degree or CPA certificate for employment because of the accounting and auditing work involved. The structure of such firms is not dissimilar to that of a law firm so that there is the potential of a partnership, although you must become a CPA to be considered for selection.

In applying for a position with these firms it is important to make clear whether you are seeking an accounting or a legal position with the organization since both types of positions are offered. If you are seeking a nonlegal post, the firm will want to be sure that that is truly your desire and that they will not find themselves with a frustrated would-be lawyer on their hands.

Unions

Today unions represent almost every type of nonmanagerial activity in business, industry, and government. While all unions use lawyers on a day-to-day or occasional basis, many are finding that legally trained persons bring a depth to their administrative performance that otherwise is not possible. Coming up through the ranks is no longer a prerequisite for consideration for union posts. One of the newer membership benefits being offered by unions is a group legal service plan. In addition to the legal staff required to provide those services, there is a need for someone to administer them, and here legal training is an obvious asset.

Foundations

Because foundations are established as a result of grants or endowments, often created by wealthy individuals, for specific charitable, educational, information, or research purposes, they are not so numerous as the usual business organizations, and opportunities for legally trained persons are therefore necessarily fewer. The complexity of administration, however, offers unique possibilities for legally trained persons whose interests and abilities match the purposes of the particular organization.

A substantial portion of foundation work involves screening applications for grants and verifying the credentials of the seekers as to their ability to carry through the programs suggested. Once a grant is given, there is continual monitoring to be sure that the activities are being completed as planned. In addition to these tasks basic to the foundation concept, there is also a general management function that includes the investment and supervision of the foundation funds to obtain the income from which the grants are made. You may have to look a little harder to find these positions, but if your interests are in tune with the organization, your job satisfaction is virtually assured.

Individual Entrepreneurs

There is a long history of lawyers as entrepreneurs. Although circumstance may have been the original cause of the establishment or purchase of a business, legal training appears to provide lawyers with special abilities that are utilized very effectively in this area. The variety represented by these entrepreneurs is so vast that it is difficult to classify. There are some relatively new fields, however, that lawyers have entered in which their legal training appears to prove particularly advantageous.

One of the most recent is the high technology, venture capital company. In this type of company the entrepreneur puts up the capital to start a new business for which success is by no means guaranteed in return for stock in the new company. If the new enterprise is successful the entrepreneur will gain the return of his or her investment many times over. If the new business fails, the invested capital is lost. The ability to quickly evaluate the potential success of the venture is crucial, so that those drawn to this field usually need a background of engineering or scientific training that enables them to apply their legal training most effectively in this setting.

Lobbying is another such field. Although lobbying can be performed in a number of organizational settings, many attorneys are pursuing lobbying as a career through their own organizations. In some cases they have clients on a retainer basis, but often their activities are directed to one particular cause or interest in a group or organization at a particular point in time. Legal training is obviously an advantage in dealing with the government and its laws and regulations.

Acting as agents is a fairly new lawyer activity. Agents who serve sports and entertainment figures undertake to develop professional opportunities for their clients and often also manage their business affairs completely. Working under contract for clients, an agent arranges for the work from which the performer derives his or her income and then not only pays the bills but also arranges to invest money on the client's behalf from which future income will be received. This monopoly on the client's economic well-being is a challenge to a wide variety of lawyering skills if it is to be performed successfully. Agents of celebrities often become well-known themselves, but their developing careers may come to be guided by an agent as well.

Consulting work is another area in which lawyers are frequently found. Consultants are individuals who have developed special knowledge in an individual field, be it broad or narrow, and who apply this knowledge for individual clients because the assignments apply to the particular expertise of the individual being consulted. The broad range of services provided are not usually available through management consultant firms. Because consulting work requires specialized knowledge, it ususally represents mid- or later-career developments except for those individuals who have acquired expertise early in their lives.

Further Possibilites

Frequently opportunities in nonlegal areas are related to or dependent upon educational credentials or work experiences outside the law, gained before, during, or after law school. Thus unusual combinations of skills may prepare someone for unusual career opportunities.

If you are uncertain of just what skills you can offer that would be useful in these nonlegal areas, you will find it useful to refer to *From Law Student to Lawyer: A Career Planning Manual*, the first book in this Career Series, with particular attention to Chapter 3. The career potential inherent in these nonlegal areas is such that you cheat only yourself if you fail to explore the possibilities thoroughly.

This exploration may suggest opportunities that do not fall neatly into the categories that have been listed. That by no means invalidates them. The possible areas listed are those in which numbers of lawyers have already developed satisfactory careers. In each, someone was there first, followed by a second, then a third person, and so on. At no time, however, have such persons limited nonlegal employment. In finding your own answers, you may simply be pushing back the horizons a bit more.

4

How to Find and Get a Nonlegal Position

Preparation

By now you probably have a feeling that obtaining a nonlegal position that will allow you to utilize the skills you have acquired in law school is going to require a different approach than you would use if you were seeking a position in legal practice. You are right. In both areas, however, more positions are probably lost through failure to do adequate homework than for any other reason.

Think of the hard work you have put in obtaining a legal education. Think of the financial costs involved. Isn't it worth an additional investment of your time and effort, as well as money for resumes, cover letters, and postage, to find the type of work you want? Besides, it's your search, and no one can do it as well as you.

There is, however, another side to the coin. Business organizations throughout the country are eagerly seeking bright new people who will make a definite contribution. They have no central clearinghouse available through which they may seek you out, so they must depend upon your contacting them concerning the qualifications you offer.

Because there is no organized system for bringing you and the prospective employer together, you will need your own system if you are to conduct an effective search. The first step is to decide how you will limit your search. The reason is apparent when you contemplate the more than 18,000 businesses which are listed in a national directory such as *Poor's Directory of Corporations*.

There are a number of possible ways by which you can set your own limits. If you have already decided on a general area in which you would like to work, you can limit your search to those companies likely to have substantial activity in that field. Again, you may wish to limit your search geographically. Or you may wish to limit your search to a particular type of business or organization such as banks over merchandising companies, chemical companies over heavy industry, or any one of a thousand possibilities. At all times, keep in mind that you can expand or contract your search as your circumstances and the results may make advisable. Determine your priorities! Take charge of your search rather than letting your search run you.

When you have initially established the limits of your search, the next step is to undertake a research program. This step is of particular importance, for you will be limiting your search to positions matching your needs, interests, and special abilities. Thus the goal of your research program is to compile information on the employers whom you wish to seek out and to arm yourself with information concerning the individual institution that you decide you want to contact. You will find helpful suggestions for doing this in Richard N. Bolles' *What Color is Your Parachute?*

Fortunately, there are ample resource materials to which you can turn. Do not expect to find a list of prospective employers that will automatically eliminate the need for a lot of hard work on your part. An individualized job search also means an individualized research program.

The end result will be worth that effort. It will provide the basis for a personalized job search that is unlikely to be duplicated by anyone else.

One of your first references will probably be a general business directory such as *Standard and Poor's* or *Moody's*. These volumes carry a wealth of information. For example, *Standard and Poor's* provides an alphabetical listing of corporations throughout the United States and, in addition, provides for each of these corporations the address and phone number of the home office, the corporate status whether a division or subsidiary, a listing of the directors and executives, annual revenue, products produced or nature of the business, and Standard Industrial Classifications for company activities. Separate volumes provide an alphabetical listing of the corporations by their industrial classification, an alphabetical listing by state and city, and a directory of biographical information on the directors and executives listed.

These volumes are quite expensive so that it is unlikely one would wish to purchase one's own. You should be able to find them, however, in any sizable public library, college or university library, law school library, placement office career libarary, or business school library. If all else fails, you might inquire of your local bank to see if they have a copy that you might use.

A very useful volume is the *Guide to American Directories*. This volume is broken down by subject categories in each of which the directory title, publisher's address, and cost are provided. For example, let us suppose that you are specifically interested in banking and financial activities. Under that listing, you would find an entry for the *American Bank Attorneys* together with the address of the publisher and the cost of the volume. As the cost of this particular volume is relatively inexpensive, you might wish to order your own copy from the publisher. What will undoubtedly amaze you is the tremendous number of such specialized directories. There is almost certainly one that pertains to your own interests, no matter how specialized.

Still another valuable reference is the *Encyclopedia of Associations*. Business enterprises in the same area of activity will usually have a trade association, which will be listed in the *Encyclopedia*. Most associations can provide you with background information in the field, and you can garner much valuable information from the pages of their publications and other career material which they may have. A general letter of inquiry as to the availability of such materials is all that is needed is to get the ball rolling.

Rounding out this roster of background materials is the *Business Periodicals Index*. Arranged by subject matter, this volume provides the address and subscription rate for all periodicals in specialized fields. You may want to consider a subscription to one or more of these publications. To make it easy, the *Index* provides the name and address of the publisher and the annual subscription rate. Be alert, however, for possible duplication with other directory listings.

At the end of your basic research, you should not only have immediately available to you the names and addresses of specific prospective employers with whom you are interested in making contact, but also some basic background information on the institution. In addition, you will also be collecting from business publications, general industry information and details on current problems and similar important matters that will be invaluable to you in approaching your market most effectively.

As you develop your prospect list, you may also find yourself particularly interested in several specific organizations. In many instances, you can obtain much more complete information directly from the organization itself. There are two possibilities.

Because these organizations are interested in attracting the most capable administration and management personnel that they can get, many produce a special recruiting publication. It will provide information on the organization's activities, the attractions of its particular location, and it may suggest various functions in which administrative and management personnel are currently employed. Such a publication will serve to give you concrete information as to whether the type of activity in which you are interested is a substantial one within the organization, and it may also suggest new and interesting areas which you would be eager to explore.

It is the custom of most of the organizations that produce these publications to see that a copy is forwarded to the university placement office, even if they will not have interviewers on campus. If you cannot locate such a publication at that source, try writing directly for information on administrative and management careers within the organization.

Still another source of information for corporations is the annual stockholders' report. Although this is obviously a publication intended for a wider readership, nevertheless it can give you a wealth of background information which will be useful from the moment of your initial contact with that company.

Organization

One of the goals of your research program was the development of your own listing of potential employers. Names and addresses alone, however, will not be enough for an effective job search. What you will require is a system for organizing the information you will be acquiring.

What kind of information do you need to know? Any and all that may contribute to a productive contact and promote more effective interviewing. Although there is really no limit to the possible data which can be collected, there are a few basic requirements which you will certainly wish to meet.

First is the name of the individual within the business organization who will receive your initial contact. Try to make it the head of the special area in which you are specifically interested. If you are uncertain about the area, then use the head of personnel. If you have been unable to locate this information in one of your directories, call the company headquarters and ask the switchboard operator for the name of the individual you wish to reach. In the latter event, be sure to ask for the spelling of the name and the exact title. Mistakes on these points can be damaging.

Certainly you will want to collect information on the nature of the company's business. There is a sound reason for this. You are asking the business organization to be interested in your qualifications with a view to possible employment. Is it not reasonable that they should expect that you would have taken the time and trouble to find out about the products or services of their organization?

As you develop your information, keep asking yourself three questions: What are this employer's need or problems and how might I contribute to solutions? How can my skills solve *their* problems? and How will hiring me save them money?

A word of caution, however. Hiring you will not be the salvation of the company. That is not your goal at this point. Rather, what you are seeking to do is find ways in which your employment will be an asset to the organization. For example, how can your legal training enable you to do the job more quickly, more thoroughly, more profitably for the organization?

Essentially this will be basic information, but you undoubtedly will wish to flesh it out with further background that will assist you at the interview. You may add newspaper and magazine clippings, the brochures mentioned in the previous section, and all sorts of information that may come your way in the course of your research which will serve to make you as familiar with the individual organization as possible.

If you possibly can, locate present or past employees of the organization and interview them for information concerning the insights they have gained through their employment. Keep in mind that you will encounter differences of opinion that should not cloud your own judgments, and concentrate on the facts you get.

As you perhaps can detect by now, your individual files may become quite voluminous. How may you best organize this material? The most practical answer would appear to be one or more loose-leaf notebooks which, if you do not already possess them, can be inexpensively obtained. The reason for the notebooks is that they permit you to add and subtract material as it seems necessary. You can also easily arrange your files in a sequence which is easiest for you to use, whether it be geographical or alphabetical. The notebooks are also easily transported to a library where you are doing your background research.

By allowing one full sheet or more if needed for each prospective employer, you leave yourself room to make notations regarding dates of contact, individuals spoken to, and your own observations and comments. The size of the loose-leaf page also makes it easy to enter additional information as you develop it.

Before your basic research and development of a roster of prospective employers is completed, you will also want to develop a resume and basic cover letter. All too many people get the cart before the horse. They want to start writing the resume before they have analyzed their qualifications. It is particularly important in approaching the business community, as opposed to a law office, simply because completion of a legal education will be only one of a number of qualifications in which the organization will be interested, as opposed to the law office for which your legal education is of critical interest.

The business organization will want to know other aspects of your education and training that will be pertinent to job performance, the types of work experience that you may have had and the duties and responsibilities involved. As you jot down the various items, use your imagination to determine how the experiences that you have had would contribute to the business career you are seeking. Even if your work experience has been only in low-level jobs, see if the pattern does not indicate ambition, drive, eagerness for education, and ability to get along with others. Make a note of your conclusions. Much more on these techniques will be found in *From Law Student to Lawyer: A Career Planning Manual,* which is part of this Career Series.

Once you have assembled all of this information, you will then be able to decide on how your material should be arranged within your resume. You can find dozens of samples of good resumes in any job-hunting guide. There is no "correct" formula. What you seek to do is to provide information about *you* and your *qualifications* in a manner that will best call attention to the most important points at the very outset. A one-page resume is the ideal, but in most circumstances it should not be more than two pages.

Once you are satisfied with the arrangement of information, it is time to get the resume in final form ready for proofreading and printing. At this point it is a foolish economy to print too few. It will be cheaper to purchase 500 copies and discard almost all rather than go through the expense of several reprintings as the job search proceeds.

Most people tend to underestimate the number of resumes that they will want to use. Investigate the availability of word processing for this task. This equipment can greatly simplify the work of adapting resumes and creating personalized cover letters.

One important factor to keep in mind is that your resume may be read initially by someone in the personnel department of the organization who is responsible for recruiting administrative and management personnel. As the personnel office is often a major stumbling block for legally trained persons seeking business careers, let us talk about the persons in them and how you may obtain their assistance in your own search. This is probably easiest by putting yourself in the other person's shoes.

A major factor that turns off highly trained applicants such as legally trained individuals is the seemingly impersonal attitude created by the personnel department of the organization and the paperwork necessary to handle the recruitment, record keeping, and related functions. Consider your own job search program and the amount of paperwork involved and multiply this many times over, and you will have some idea of the difficulties faced by personnel administrators in an organization with many employees.

The individuals you will be talking to in personnel measure their effective job performance by their ability to recruit and to channel into appropriate slots the most qualified employees to fill company needs. Thus it is in their best interests, as well as yours, to communicate as freely and fully as possible. For example, can you imagine the suggestions which you might receive if at some point in your conversation you were to say something along the lines of, "Initially, I was considering a nonlegal position in the contract administration area. However, I would be interested in your thoughts on other alternatives in the organization you can suggest, areas where my background and experience could best be utilized." As you can see, this type of approach gives you and the company representative a common goal, to find a position which will use your talents to the fullest and thereby offer the best possibility for advancement.

Keep in mind that your resume will be read by someone experienced in doing just that, and able, therefore, to glean the important information efficiently and rapidly. You will also be interviewed by a person experienced in employment interviewing. In fact, the individual to whom you speak may well have trained the management level persons of the organization in the art of effective interviewing so that they also may do the best job in attracting qualified individuals to the posts under their jurisdiction. Personnel people, because of their experience, can be strong allies in your search for a position that you will be happy with and where you can perform most effectively—but only if you let them.

If the organization is small and does not have a personnel department or if you can make direct contact, your initial interview may be with a management person in the area of interest you have indicated.

Even as you have been developing your prospect files of employer prospects, you will have started the third step of your job search program. That is the preparation of the general pattern for your cover letter. The resume itself is of necessity a somewhat formal document. The cover letter is essentially your sales pitch. It need be only three paragraphs long.

In the first paragraph, tell the organization why you are specifically contacting it. Look at your research notes for clues. Is it the type of activity that has particular appeal? Did the stockholders' report indicate a dynamic and aggressive management team? Is it because of the growth potential of the company? The particular reason you use is not so important as the evidence it provides that you have been specifically interested in that particular organization enough to find out something about it. Your geographic preferences, for example, would probably not be pertinent. What you want is something about the company that made you want to contact them.

The next paragraph should call to their attention your resume and particular qualifications for the opportunity that you seek. *It should make clear that you are applying for a nonlegal position* even though you may call attention to aspects of your legal education that might particularly relate to effective job performance.

The third paragraph should specifically state the reason for your communication. "I am interested in arranging an interview with a view to possible employment," may seem too direct but it clearly states the purpose of your contact and is therefore more likely to produce action. The final sentence of this last paragraph should indicate an address or telephone number where you can be reached, or preferably both. Do not worry that this information also appears on your resume. Its purpose on the resume is information; in the cover letter it is action-oriented.

Since the cover letter must be individually typewritten, addressed to a specific person, and varied at least in the first paragraph by your differing reasons for contact, production of such letters may seem an insurmountable task. Keep in mind, however, that it can proceed as your research work proceeds and new contacts are developed. Furthermore, you can divide the project into manageable segments. For example, five letters a week might be a manageable number; a hundred letters a week might be impossible. This is where a word processor can make even a hundred letters a week an easy task.

Execution

Procrastination is the arch enemy of every job search program. As early as you possibly can in your law school career, you should begin the development of your research program, your resume, and your cover letter. As has already been indicated, your letters and resumes can start going out even though your research program is only partially completed.

Don't worry if this seems far too far in advance of your availability for full-time employment. Larger organizations plan their recruiting for management trainee spots well in advance of the development of specific openings. They know it will take a great deal of time to get together the persons they wish to employ. Of course, it will also take you considerable time to complete your total job-search program. Once your well-thought-out program is underway, requests for interviews are certain to develop.

Before those interviews you will want to refresh your memory regarding the particular company by reviewing the files which you have researched and developed. In addition, you should take time to sit down with your resume and review it in light of the kind of questions you may be asked.

You are quite likely to find that the skilled nonlegal employment interviewer goes about the interview in a manner quite different than that used by the law office employer for whom the practice of law is the major activity, not interviewing. In part the difference in approach will also reflect the basic goal of the interviewer. The law office interviewer is seeking to determine what kind of a lawyer you will make, whereas the business interviewer is seeking to determine not only the skills you bring to the job but also the type of person you are in terms of your potential for future advancement within the organization.

Because the approach is likely to be different, it is wise to look at the types of questions you are probably going to be asked. The first thing that will probably amaze you is the range the interview will cover.

Why this range? The interviewer is seeking within the relatively short space of the interview to get to know you as a person. Your "paper credentials" are before him or her and these can be independently verified. Getting to know you as a person in a limited amount of time is far more difficult, so the interviewer will have organized that time to obtain as much intangible information as possible.

Of course, you can expect questions concerning your educational background, but they will not concentrate solely on your legal training. Don't be surprised if the interviewer asks you which subjects you liked best in elementary school, or, conversely, what you liked least. When any work experience which you may have had is discussed, anticipate being asked what you feel you did best and where you felt you were less effective. Questions as to how you felt about teachers and supervisors are almost routine. Don't be surprised if you are asked to describe your parents' personalities, or the differences you see between yourself and any brothers and sisters you have. Obviously, such questions are somewhat difficult to respond to off the cuff so that by thinking them through, you are better prepared to respond.

Keep in mind that this will not be an inquisition. Rather, the aim of the interviewer is to discover your reaction to the people and activities you have encountered in your life. The facts about you are in your resume and the application form you probably completed before the interview. The interviewer is seeking information about the kind of person you are, how you relate to others, and what special strengths you feel you have. Even the best resume and application cannot supply that.

In fact, the more skilled the interviewer, the more you will find that you enjoy the interview. It will be a conversation, a conversation about you, and who doesn't enjoy that? With a skilled interviewer, however, there will be no doubt as to who is in charge of the interview.

The second aim of the interviewer will be to develop information concerning skills that would enhance your performance in the position which you are seeking. Obviously, this gives you opportunity to discuss how your legal education would be applicable. In addition, the analysis you did in preparing to write your resume will be most useful. Think of this not only in terms of skills applicable to the position for which you are applying, but also in terms of future flexiblity to meet the requirements of advanced positions with greater responsibilities.

Keep your mind open not only to those tangible skills you have but also to those intangible ones. For example, Are you a leader? How do you deal with problems? How do your peers react to you? How do you deal with "difficult" people? Answers to questions such as these will probably highlight skills you had only dimly perceived before.

A single interview within a business organization is unlikely to result in an employment offer. If the initial interview is with someone in the personnel department, no decision will be reached until you have talked with one or more individuals under whose supervision you would be launching your business career. The questions may vary, but you will probably find that the essential approach remains the same.

You have undoubtedly heard that you will have your most effective interview if you relax. This is sound advice since none of us appears at our best when we are nervous or tense. Yet most people find it difficult to relax under the tensions of an interview. Thankfully there is something you can do. The more you know about the organization with which you are interviewing and the more you have analyzed your own abilities, interests, and future plans, the easier the interview process becomes for you.

None of us has escaped the experience of having a hostess introduce us with a flat "Jane, meet Joe." Remember how you have struggled to establish rapport without any information to start the conversation rolling with. On the other hand, remember the host or hostess who introduced you in such a fashion as, "Jane, I'd like you to meet Joe, who is really into skiing. Jane has just returned from a week's skiing vacation at Aspen." Remember how smoothly and easily the conversation went.

Translating that experience into business terms, your most successful employment interviews will be those in which you know both your market and your product. Acquiring that knowledge is not easy.

You may be somewhat discouraged when you contemplate the amount of research to be done, the difficult self-analysis necessary to produce a good resume, and the multitude of contacts and interviews you will have. Keep in mind, however, that an effective job search has as its aim the locating of a challenging and interesting position in which you can contribute to the organization all the skills and abilities you possess. Only rarely is it a one-shot deal.

Because there is no end-of-the-term grade or regular paycheck coming in to test how well your job search program is going, plan to reward yourself for maximum performance each step of the way. This reward need not be expensive. For example, it could be an hour of reading just for pleasure. Whatever you choose, all that is necessary is that it remind you that you are giving this important endeavor your best efforts at each step of the way. It will also provide a tremendous boost to your own morale, a big advantage in any job search.

Resources

Imagination Prodders

When you start looking for a position in an area that is completely unbounded by routine job descriptions, your best friend is a lively imagination inhibited only by the application of your particular skills and interests. In other words, use your creativity.

Many find that term disturbing, if not frightening. To demonstrate that most people have this quality, even though they may not recognize it as such, a simple test was devised several years ago and has appeared in several magazines. Imagine you are faced with decorating your room or apartment that has a wall with a small awkward window in the upper lefthand corner. How many ways can you think to turn this liability into an asset?

Immediately a number of drapery arrangements may suggest themselves to you. Keep on. For the moment, forget cost and feasibility. Soon ideas will begin to flow. What about an Indian open-worked screen to cover the window? Or an open-weave basket as a disguise? Perhaps a bookcase in which the window is used to provide light for an exotic plant collection. And so on.

You can probably come up with at least a dozen more ideas. *Then* the process of weeding out those ideas that are unsuitable by reason of cost or feasibility begins. So it is with your review of the nonlegal job market.

When it comes to using the same creative approach to the job search, your greatest difficulty may be in imagining the various types of positions that may be available in an organization in which your legal training might be a particular qualification, even though it may not be listed as a job requirement. How can you overcome this?

In the *Dictionary of Occupational Titles*, published by the U.S. Department of Labor, it is suggested that those with an undergraduate degree in history might find work in museum, library and archival sciences occupations. Two occupations are listed in this category, that of museum curator and one an additional classification for museum technicians. That is all. There is no mention of the person who must be responsible for the transportation regulations affecting the shipment of delicate and priceless objects to and from the museum. There is no mention of the individual who must be responsible for overseeing the insurance contracts covering the special and permanent exhibits. There is no mention of the individual who will be responsible for the financial records of the institution. With some additional thought, you can undoubtedly add at least a dozen opportunities for legally trained persons in a museum setting even if these might be lumped into a single adminstrative post in a small museum. All of these would be spots in which your particular background and legal training might be applicable if this were your field of interest.

The positions listed in the following pages are intended as jumping-off places for your own imagination. They are not job descriptions as such, but rather, in most cases, descriptions of fairly easily recognized alternative careers for lawyers. You may find a few that will be interesting to you. If so, stop and imagine a potential career pattern that might start or emerge at the given point indicated. If you are still not satisfied with the possibilities that you find listed, then use your imagination further to develop new ideas and possibilities.

Once you have located one or two particular career areas that seem to suit your interests and abilities, then it is time to begin your thorough research into that particular area and its potential for you.

A Review of the *Wall Street Journal* Want Ads for Nonlegal Positions

The following is a day-by-day review of want ads during an entire month appearing in *The Wall Street Journal* in which legal background and training would appear to have been an advantage in applying for the position. The *Journal* is published Monday through Friday, and the following listing is consecutive.

For most persons these positions will represent second- or third-step career developments. Do any of these positions sound interesting to you? Can you think of other types of positions these organizations might offer where your particular background would be an asset? Note the frequency with which these ads appeared in relationship to those in traditional practice.

Once you have reviewed the list for types of organizations and positions that may be of interest to you, use it to practice defining how a legal education might be a particular qualification for employer consideration. What types of duties might the position call for? Why would your legal education permit you to do the job faster, easier, or cheaper? What types of problems might your legal training help you avert? This type of analysis will be crucial when you are applying for the position or positions in which you are really interested, and the more skillfully you do it, the more it will be to your advantage.

Day	*Type of Employer*	*Type of Work*
Day 1	State	Supervision of savings and loan Associations
	State	Supervision of credit unions
	Bank	Commercial loans
	Real estate company	Loan producer
	Corporation	Tax planner
	Bank	Supervision of loans to petroleum and natural resources industries
	Company	Personnel, including benefits
	Investment Company	Bond portfolio management
	Bank	Farm manager for trust real estate
	Real estate trust	Financial management
	Manufacturer	General management

Six lawyer positions were listed this day, including two openings for patent lawyers.

Day 2	Savings and loan	Mortgage management
	Bank holding corporation	Commercial lending
	Association management firm	Government relations
	Financial services company	Real estate security
	Manufacturer	Organization development and compensation manager

Three lawyer positions were listed this day, including two openings for patent lawyers.

Day 3 University   General administration
       Title company   Management
       Oil company   General management
       Appliance   Sales and marketing
         manufacturer

One lawyer position was listed this day.

Day 4 Bank   Commercial loan
       Financial services   Real estate securities
         company
       Manufacturer   Corporate planner

One lawyer position was listed this day.

Day 5 Developer   Leasing agent
       Industrial company   Employee benefits planning
       Utility   Rate analysis
       Developer   General management
       Health care company   Financial packaging for promo-
                                tion, construction, and opera-
                                tion of units
       Bank   Foreign business development
       Savings and loan   Mortgage area
       Consulting firm   General management
       Government agency   Land pollution management

Eight lawyer positions were listed this day, including an opening for a patent lawyer.

Day 6 Industrial corporation Personnel and industrial relations
       City Central Business   Development
         District
       Marketing company   Credit management
       Financial controls   General management
       Bank   Trust field
       Federal agency   General utilities management
       Consulting firm   Investment management
       Developer   Shopping center leasing
       Mortgage company   Mortgage management

Bank   Commercial loans

Three lawyer positions were listed this day, including one opening for a patent lawyer and one requiring engineering background.

Day 7	Manufacturer	Technical employment recruiting
	Association	Membership sales
	Company	Workmens' compensation self-insurance management
	Bank	Trust investment management

Two lawyer positions were listed this day.

Day 8	Bank	International operations
	Company	Land development, contract management and investment
	Real estate organization	Organization-leasing management

Two lawyer positions were listed this day.

| Day 9 | Consulting firm | Municipal finance management |

One lawyer position was listed this day.

Day 10	Manufacturer	Customs administration
	Manufacturer	Industrial grievances
	Finance company	Mobile-home financing
	Corporate lending group	Commercial loans
	Manufacturer	Tax compliance in planning
	Manufacturer	Compensation management
	Real estate organization	Commercial loans
	Manufactureer	International operations management

Three lawyer positions were listed this day, including one opening for a patent lawyer.

Day 11	Oil company	Community development management
	Investment company	Loan marketing management
	Bank	Bond portfolio management
	Bank	Commercial loans

Developer	Lending management
Corporation	Business planning
Bank	Commercial loans
Corporation	Tax management
Developer	Leasing agent
Bank	General management
Developer	General management
Manufacturer	Labor relations
Manufacturer	Financial management

No lawyer positions were listed this day.

Day 12 Real estate firm   Management of commercial property acquisitions in analyzing acquisitions

No lawyer positions were listed this day.

Day 13 City   Economic development
        Real estate   Marketing representative investment company
        Developer   Investment syndicator

No lawyer positions were listed this day.

Day 14 Corporation   General management

No lawyer positions were listed this day.

Day 15 Minority business   New business development, development firm

Corporation	Labor relations
Corporation	Insurance management
Leasing corporation	Lease credit management
Financial services company	Secured business loans
Leasing company	Marketing
Manufacturer	Credit management
Insurance company	Marketing management
Mortgage company	Mortgage placement
Company	Labor relations
Real estate company	Public affairs management
Bank	Investment advisory services
Corporation	Regional tax compliance

Corporation	Tax return preparation
Hospital	Fund-raising

Two lawyer positions were listed this day.

Day 16	Health care service company	Tax management
	Developer	Property manager
	Company	Labor relations
	Merchandising company	Site selection and lease negotiation
	Corporation	Labor relations
	Bank holding corporation	Commercial lending
	Real estate investment trust	General management
	Corporation	Executive and international compensation
	Retailer	Tax management

No lawyer positions were listed this day.

Day 17	Bank	Trust investment

No lawyer positions were listed this day.

Day 18	Company	Salary administration
	CPA firm	International tax management

No lawyer positions were listed this day.

Day 19	State	Administration environmental controls
	Manufacturer	Labor relations
	Development foundation	Fund-raising

One lawyer position was listed this day.

Day 20	Consulting firm	Compensation area
	Commercial lending organization	General management
	Company	Tax management
	CPA firm	Tax research, planning, and review

City	General management
University	Development and public affairs
Bank	Trust and estate administration
Bank holding corporation	Commercial lending
Corporation	International compensation management
Industrial credit company	General credit managemen
State	Administration of environmental controls agency
Corporation	Industrial relations
Corporation	Industrial relations
Corporation	Industrial relations

One patent lawyer position was listed this day.

Day 21	Bank	Commercial lending
	Bank	Investment management
	Bank	Trust administration
	Bank	Trust administration
	Bank	Commercial lending
	Bank	Operations
	Bank	International operations
	Bank	International operations
	Bank	Commercial loans
	Manufacturer	Industrial relations
	Bank	Bond portfolio management
	Manufacturer	Credit management
	Corporation	Compensation management
	Corporation	Industrial relations

Five lawyer positions were listed this day, including one for an attorney-physicist.

Day 22	Company	Commercial finance sales

No lawyer positions were listed this day.

Nonlegal Positions Accepted by Law Graduates Reported in the 1981 Employment Report of the National Association for Law Placement

While *The Wall Street Journal* advertises positions for experienced individuals, the reports of students graduating from law school who accepted nonlegal positions give clues as to how such careers began, as well as providing evidence of imaginative approaches to the marketplace used by many. The following listings from the 1981 Employment Survey of the NALP provides evidence of such in but a single year.

The survey, compiled from data submitted by 134 of the 171 ABA-approved law schools invited to participate, defined the employment status of 23,352 graduates.

Once again, when you have reviewed the list for positions of potential interest, use it to practice your skills in analyzing why your legal training would make you better qualified than others who might be under consideration. Could you do the work more rapidly and at less cost? What potential problems might you be able to avert? It is better to make your trial and error here than in that really important interview.

Nonlegal Positions in Business Concerns

Assistant personnel manager
Engineering department
Regulatory affairs director
Human resources management supervisor
Commercial real estate land man
Computer analyst
Consultant, employee benefits
Corporate regulatory affairs

Airlines management
Assistant plant manager
EEO specialist, personnel
Labor relations department
Hospital administrator
Farm Bureau Federation lobbyist
Corporation lobbyist

Trucking corporation manager

Contracts department
Energy relations manager
Industry manager
Industrial relations manager

Community affairs director of a TV station
Consultant
Contract negotiator
University development program
Immigration services director
Assistant to the president
Financial consulting
Geologist
Invention disclosure analyst
LEXIS employee

Manufacturing company manager
Oil and gas consultant

Training and development
Bookstore owner
Private consultant
Rock music promotion

Senior financial analyst
Senior underwriter

Stockbroker
Title examiner

Orthopedic surgeon
Pension administrator
Research chemist
Office building selling and
    leasing
Senior research analyst
Shopping center development
    director
Technical writer

Nonlegal Positions in Nonprofit Concerns

Center for reproductive health
Black Officers association
Television news reporter

Nurses association
Public administration
United Way

Nonlegal Positions in Government

Campaign manager
Peace Corps

Real estate broker
State Ombudsperson for institu-
    tionalized elderly

Office of the mayor
Press secretary to a guber-
    natorial candidate
State legislature

Nonlegal Positions in Academe

Assistant to the president
Consulting assistant professor
Elementary school teacher

Fund-raising development
High school teacher

European internship program
Paralegal and legal secretaries
    teacher
School administration

Computer research
Coordinator of judicial affairs
Fellowship, juvenile law and
    development
State department of education
State university personnel
    manager
Nonlegal teaching
Public school truant officer

Teacher, public school, legal
    courses only

Corporate Nonlegal Positions

In response to the NALP survey mentioned in the preceding section, many of the corporations supplied lists of positions currently being filled by legally-trained persons outside their legal departments. Still others added lists of positions where it was felt an individual with legal training would be a particular asset. Although not identified by name, all of the following corporations are among *Fortune*'s 500.

An Oil and Gas Producer

Manager, government relations

Manager, employee relations

Superintendent of personnel and training

Division land representative

Senior staff, land representation

District land representative

Land representative

Senior representative, negotiations and contracts

Senior contracts analyst

Associate contracts analyst

Senior staff coordinator

Chief right-of-way agent

Petroleum engineer

Assistant general manager, administration

Division manager, marketing

Field I representative

Assistant manager, financial reporting

Systems analyst

Senior project chemical engineer

Assistant to the manager

Manager, labor relations

Supervisor, employee relations

Chief land representative

Division assistant, land representation

Assistant to the division land representative

Supervisor, land records

Associate land representative

Contract supervisor

Contracts analyst

General manager, real estate development

Assistant general manager, fleet planning

Supervisor of budget

Geophysicist

General manager, marketing

Division supervisor, credit sales

Marketing representative

Supervisor, petrochemical accounting

Manager, financial planning

Environmental specialist

A Wood and Paper Corporation

Tax attorney

Senior tax attorney

Director, environmental affairs

Vice president, governmental affairs

Manager, planning and communications (employee benefits)

Director, equal opportunity affairs

Director, labor relations

Manager, labor relations

Director, real estate facilities

Manager, real estate facilities

Manager, marketing

Vice President, planning and control

Manager, health and welfare plans

Manager, retirement and savings plans

Regional manager, equal opportunity affairs

Director, loss prevention

Manager, loss prevention

Director, risk management

Manager, risk management

A Food Products Corporation

Manager, employee benefits

Supervisor, employee planning

Manager, industrial relations

Supervisor, industrial relations

Manager, employment opportunities programs

Manager, government affairs

Supervisor, taxes (state and/or U.S.)

Secretary/assistant secretary

A Merchandising Corporation

National merchandise manager

Assistant buyer

Staff assistant

Director of employee benefits

Merchandise controller

Assistant marketing manager

Manager, insurance department

A Manufacturing Corporation

Director, public relations

product information manager

Public relations assistant

Real estate insurance manager

Credit manager

Credit analyst

Cash manager
Treasurer
Comptroller
Internal auditor
Purchasing manager
Traffic manager
Trucking supervisor
Labor relations manager
Benefit plan administrator
Employment manager
Safety director

Office services manager
Accounting manager
Internal audit manager
Payroll manager
Buyer
Rate specialist
Rail supervisor
Benefits manager
EEO coordinator
Recruiter

A Manufacturing Corporation with Highly Diverse Divisions and Subsidiaries

Contract administrator

Manager, contracts and
proposals
Manager, business affairs

Manager, taxes
Administrator, copyright and
permissions acquisitions
Manager, contracts

Division vice president,
technical programs
Vice president, Washington
office
Administrator, technical
relations
Director, electronic components
licensing
Manager, claims branch
Manager, federal income tax
President, three subsidiaries or
divisions
Manager, marketing affairs

Manager, contracts
management
Purchase subcontracting
administrator
Manager, business and talent
affairs
Manager, permissions
Administrator, subsidiary rights

Division vice president,
international
Manager, labor relations

Manager, consumer affairs

Vice president, licensing

Claims field representative

Tax research specialist
Director, taxes
Senior data processing aide

Senior member of the engineering staff

Manager, employment and
communications
Manager, consumer services

Manager, test development and
quality

A Rubber Manufacturer

Director, equal opportunity
programs
Director, corporate security
Director, government relations
Executive vice president and
general manager
President and director
Special assignment
Buyer

Audit representative
Manager, international
transportation
Latin America manager
Manager, real estate
administration
Senior union relations
representative

Director, vinyl monomer supply

Director, employee relations
Director, labor relations
Vice president, employee
relations
Assistant treasurer
Product engineer
Associate research and develop-
ment scientist
Real estate field representative
Regional manager

Store manager
Product manager

A Food Manufacturer

Vice president, controller

Director, employee relations
Director, corporate taxes

Vice president, government
relations
Director, technical services

A Pharmaceutical Manufacturer

Director, taxation

Manager, corporate compliance
and agency relations
Manager, regulatory
compliance

Director, corporate labor
relations
Coordinator, regulatory
compliance

An Oil and Gas Corporation

Manager, investigations

Manager, protective services

Security advisor

Corporate secretary

Assistant corporate secretary

Government relations advisor

Manager, labor relations

Labor relations advisor

Division advisor, labor and safety

Tax agent

Property tax advisor

Contracts administrator

Joint interests administrator

Sales manager

General manager

Manager, domestic or foreign gas

Supervisor, contract and FTC regulations

Negotiations coordinator

Land supervisor

Senior land specialist

Land representative or agent

Suggested Readings

The following list of books will serve to start your search. As you will note, most of the entries will offer suggestions for further information sources in addition to the potential employers that are listed. If you have decided on specific areas to pursue, take advantage of these additional references.

There are no articles from periodicals listed. Until recently, nonlegal careers had received scant attention from publishers. Today that is changing and for the latest references available, check with your law school placement director who will be maintaining a file of these.

Although the publications are grouped by headings, there is a great deal of inevitable crossover. Therefore, feel free to range widely to locate the material that would be most useful to you.

The Legal Profession

Opportunities in Law Careers, Gary A. Munneke (VGM Career Horizons, 1981).

Although this book was written with a prelaw audience in mind, it presents, in readable form, an excellent overview of the variety and types of legal opportunities open to law school graduates.

Career Planning and Job Search

What Color is Your Parachute? rev. ed., Richard N. Bolles (Ten Speed Press, 1982).

Although this book does not deal with lawyers specifically, it is rapidly becoming a classic in career planning and job search. The principles it presents are sound and can be used by any student to advantage.

After Law School? Finding the Job in a Tight Market, Saul Miller (Little Brown & Company, 1978).

Written by a former placement director, this book provides specific guidelines for law students seeking their first legal position. Not only is the text full of information, but extensive resource material is provided to aid in a job search.

The Complete Job Search Handbook: All the Skills You Need to Get Any Job and Have a Good Time Doing It, Howard Figler, ed. (Holt Rinehart and Winston, 1979).

This is another book written for the general reader, but it contains valuable emphasis on self-assessment skills and their application to the job search.

One on One: Win the Interview, Win the Job, Theodore Pettus (Random House, 1981).

Everything you need to know about how to set up an interview, how to prepare for it, how to dress, how to handle yourself, and how not to make self-defeating mistakes.

Put Your Degree to Work: A Career Planning and Job Hunting Guide for the New Professional, Marcia R. Fox (W. W. Norton & Company, 1979).

A down-to-earth approach to the professional job search. An outstanding book, this job-hunter's guide includes comprehensive chapters on everything from resumes and cover letters to career decision-making.

Sweaty Palms: The Neglected Art of Being Interviewed, H. Anthony Medley (Wadsworth, Inc., Lifetime Learning Publications, 1978).

An excellent book on interviewing techniques, written by an attorney for attorneys.

Business Organizations

Moody's Industrial Manual.

Moody's Public Utility Manual.

Moody's Banks and Finance Manual.

Moody's Transportation Manual.

Published annually by Moody's Investors Service, Inc. These manuals provide information on most corporations in the United States, including mailing addresses, organizational setup, holdings, and names of corporate counsel.

Each of the manuals covers a different type of industry, as the title of each indicates. Each provides a listing with extensive background information on the corporations in that grouping. Data relating to the financial resources of each corporation is included. Keep in mind that these manuals are used extensively by banks and investors as a basis for credit and investment.

Poor's Register of Corporations (Standard & Poor's Corporation), published annually.

The variety of indexes and special codings provide additional aid in narrowing a corporate law department search in addition to the general directory information.

American Bank Attorneys (American Bank Attorneys, Capron Publishing Corporation), published semiannually.

This specialized directory lists only attorneys who serve as bank counsel. It is organized geographically by state, and includes biographical information in a separate section.

The magazine *Fortune* publishes annually in various issues lists of the first and second largest U.S. industrial corporations, the 50 largest

U.S. private industrial companies, the 500 largest U.S. non-industrial (service) corporations, the 500 largest foreign industrial corporations, the 50 largest industrial companies in the world, and the 100 largest foreign commercial banking corporations.

Business Organizations and Agencies Directory (Gale Research Company, 1980).

> This directory gives information on the commerce, banking, and investing industries. Listings include trade associations, organizations, government agencies, trade periodicals, specialized publishers, computerized research centers, and special libraries. There are key words and geographic indexes to names, addresses, key personnel, and telephone numbers.

Other Legal Career Choices

While the great majority of law school graduates will find their first legal positions in private practice, business organizations or government, others will begin their careers in areas that are less frequently identified by students as career possibilities, but which nevertheless offer exciting potential.

Other Choices: General Background

Legal Careers: Choices and Options, Vol. I, Betsy McCombs and Ellen Wayne, eds., Vol. II, Evelyn G. Anderson and Elaine G. Dushoff, eds. (National Association for Law Placement, 1982).

> In this work lawyers two to four years out of law school describe actual positions they have had, although the employer is not identified. Their information includes salary, job responsibilities, and advancement opportunities for positions from actuary to athletes' agent and landman to a lawyer. Over 250 sparks to the imaginations of law school graduates.

Group Legal Service Plans: Organization, Operation and Management (National Resource Center for Consumers of Legal Services, Harcourt, Brace and Jovanovich, 1981).

> This how-to book covers this type of legal services organization including suggestions, models, documents, and sample plans.

Other Choices: Directories

The Foundation Directory (Foundation Center).

This is an annual roster of foundations together with useful background information on each.

Law Teachers Directory (Association of American Law Schools).

This annual directory provides name-by-name listing of teachers at individual law schools throughout the country. For those interested in positions in this field, however, research should be preceded by reference to "The Law Faculty Hiring Process," by Jon W. Bruce and Michael I. Swygert, *Houston Law Review*, vol. 18, No. 2, January, 1981.

Encyclopedia of Associations (Gale Research Company).

This encyclopedia is updated annually and consists of five volumes: national organizations alphabetically; national organizations geographically; new associations; international associations; and research organizations. The encyclopedia contains much useful information regarding each organization's membership, structure, officers, and the like.

Guide to Religion-Based Organizations of Attorneys, Tarlton Law Library Legal Bibliography Service No. 19, Carol W. Christensen, compiler (University of Texas).

This is a helpful guide for those interested in the type of information its title implies.

Mental and Developmental Disabilities Directory of Legal Advocates (Commission on the Mentally Disabled, American Bar Association, 1982).

The directory gives 1982 listings for public and private attorneys working in this field.

Washington Lobbyists and Lawyers Directory, 5th ed., Edward Zuckerman and Robert Zuckerman (Amward Publications, 1982).

This directory, for those whose career interests lie in this direction, is invaluable in providing names and addresses for potential contact.

The Big Eight, Mark Stevens (MacMillan Publishing Company, Inc., 1981).

This is the inside story of multinational accounting firms that serve as advisors to big government, big money, and big corporations. The group competes fiercely for influence on price of gold, tax structure, inflation, standard of living, and this is the inside story.

Job Finders (Spectrum Books, Prentice-Hall, Inc).

This series of books is devoted to career opportunities in banking, energy, public relations, publishing, real estate, etc. Each book is organized so that the job seeker has an overview of the field. It includes an analysis of labor-intensive areas, and pinpoints those which are growing or declining. Networking and informational interviews are evaluated in the context of each field. Each book contains an information center which includes lists of the major professional organizations and trade associations, journals and directories, and, finally, an alphabetical list of principal employers.

Information Resources for Public Interest (Commission for the Advancement of Public Interest Consumer Organizations).

This book is for the imaginative, suggesting possible contacts useful for those interested in careers in this area.

Harvard Pro Bono/Public Interest Survey (Harvard Law School Placement Office).

This annually updated survey lists several thousand public interest and public service employment opportunities. It is arranged alphabetically by state, and includes information about current openings, salary, and application procedures.

Student Guide to Graduate Law Study Programs, Betsy McCombs and Ellen Wayne, eds. (New England School of Law, 1982).

This guide gives a comprehensive listing of graduate programs of law schools throughout the United States and gives details of requirements for admission and concentrations of courses offered.

List of Publishers

While all the books listed in the Suggested Readings should be readily available to you in school or public libraries, if you experience difficulty in locating them or wish to have a copy of your own, the following list should enable you to contact the individual publisher for information on price and availability.

American Bar Association
Order Fulfillment
750 N. Lake Shore Dr.
Chicago, IL 60611
1-312-988-5555

Amward Publications Inc.
Box 137
Washington, DC 20044
1-202-544-1141

Association of American Law
  Schools
Suite 370
1 DuPont Circle, NW
Washington, DC 20036
1-202-296-8851

Capron Publishing Corp.
P. O. Box 187
Wellesley Hills, MA 02181
1-617-235-0800

Commission for the Advancement of Public Interest Organizations
1875 Connecticut Avenue, NW
Suite 1013
Washington, DC
1-202-462-0505

Fortune Magazine
P. O. Box 8001
Trenton, NJ 08650
1-609-448-1700

Foundation Center
888 7th Avenue
New York, NY 10106
1-800-424-9836

Gale Research Co.
Book Tower
Detroit, MI 48226
1-313-961-2242

Harcourt Brace Jovanovich
757 Third Avenue
New York, NY 10017
1-212-754-3100

Harvard Law School
Harvard University Press
79 Garden Street
Cambridge, MA 02138
1-617-495-2600

Macmillan Publishing Co., Inc.
866 Third Avenue
New York, NY 10022
1-212-935-2000

Moody's Investors Service, Inc.
99 Church Street
New York, NY 10007
1-212-553-0421

National Association for Law
   Placement
Tulane Law School
New Orleans, LA 70118
1-504-865-5945

New England School of Law
154 Stuart Street
Boston, MA 02116
1-617-451-0010

Spectrum Books, Prentice Hall
   Inc.
Route 9
Englewood Cliffs, NJ 07632
1-201-592-2000

Standard & Poor's
345 Hudson Street
New York, NY 10014
1-212-248-2525

University of Texas School of
   Law
2500 Red River
Austin, TX 78705
1-512-471-5151

Index

Join the Law Student Division of the ABA

APPLICATION

Name _____
        Last   First   Middle

Street _____ City _____ State _____ Zip _____

Law School _____ City _____

	Birth Date			Law School Entry		Prospective Graduation Date	
Month	Day	Year		Month	Year	Month	Year

As a law student member of the ABA, I will abide by its Constitution and By-Laws.

Signature _____ Date _____

☐ Enclosed is my membership fee for $10.00, which includes an allocation of $2.75 for the *ABA Journal* and $2.50 for the *Student Lawyer*.

☐ Enclosed is $3.00 more for membership in the Section of Economics of Law Practice.

Send check and application to:
Member Records, ABA, 750 N. Lake Shore Dr., Chicago, IL 60611

Office Use Only:	☐ ☐	☐ ☐	☐ ☐
	NUMERIC STATE CODE	ALPHA STATE CODE	LAW SCHOOL CODE

A Publication Program for the 21st Century

SYSTEMATIZE YOUR PRACTICE

Docket Control Systems for Lawyers

The most effective means to avoid malpractice claims is a strict docket control system, and this manual will help you institute a monitoring system appropriate to your legal practice.

How to Create-A-System for the Law Office

This manual will help you create systems for collections, divorces, incorporations, adoptions, personal injury litigations, and many other common legal tasks.

Retrieval Systems for Lawyers

Subtitled *How to Index and Store Research and Other Office Created Documents for Future Use*, this guide will introduce you to techniques for preserving research and retrieving it for use with new clients.

Style Manual

Standardize the form, content, arrangement, and style of your legal documents. This booklet will help you systematize such facets of document preparation as size, spacing, paragraphing, and filing.

Model Accounting System

The purpose of this guide is to show lawyers how to systematize their accounting procedures, and it will enable you to control and to compare income and expenses professionally.

The Lawyer's Handbook

Over 100,000 attorneys have used the *Handbook* to help streamline their office systems. Supplemented regularly.

Simplified Accounting Systems and Concepts for Lawyers

Reveals the problems caused by inefficient bookkeeping, explains and illustrates effective bookkeeping systems for the smaller firm, and offers a standard chart of accounts.

Management of a Family Law Practice

Procedures for systematizing a divorce practice, minimizing collection problems, and introducing clients to your services.

TECHNOLOGY AND YOU

Choosing and Using Computers

To improve your law practice. Crucial information for small firms on microcomputer hardware and software.

LOCATE

Containing entries for hundreds of software packages, this directory will inform you about the suppliers of law-office computer applications and software in your area. Updated annually.

Word Processing Equipment

A basic illustrated guide to help you understand the operation of automatic typewriters, evaluate your needs, and select a suitable machine.

Planning for Computers

Intended for medium and large firms wishing to evaluate their data processing needs and update their capabilities.

Telephone Equipment for the Law Office

An introduction to the telephone and facsimile systems now available to the law office. Updated edition of *Communications Handbook for Attorneys*.

BE ADVISED

Your New Lawyer

The complete legal employer's guide to recruitment, development, and management of new lawyers.

Legal Fees and Representation Agreements

Easy-to-use models for written client/lawyer and counsel/associated counsel agreements.

Law Office Staff Manual

Model policies and procedures for the general administration of the law office.

Model Partnership Agreement

A partnership agreement focusing on the needs of an office with two to ten lawyers.

Working with Legal Assistants

This two-volume set is an indispensable source of systems, techniques, and ideas for the use of legal assistants throughout the practice of law.

How to Avoid Being Sued by Your Client

Describes numerous areas of potential liability, discusses preventive measures, and analyzes special insurance coverages.

The Best of Legal Economics

The 46 articles in this collection offer a comprehensive overview of the latest techniques in law office management and organization.

How to Start and Build a Law Practice

Now in its fifth printing, this volume by Jay Foonberg confronts the initial problems you will have to face in building a successful practice.

New Tricks for Old Dogs

Benefit from the advice of numerous attorneys who have developed procedures for solving a variety of everyday tasks and problems.

Financial Management of Law Firms
Management Controls and Reporting
Profit Planning and Budgeting for Law Firms

The first of these three related books deals with financial planning in general. The second discusses management controls and the reporting needed to exercise them. The third provides a step-by-step approach to instituting profit planning.

Law Office Organization

The classic work on the subject, now reissued.

Members of the Economics of Law Practice Section receive a 50% discount on many of the above books. For their $17.50 membership, they also receive a subscription to *Legal Economics*—a bimonthly magazine devoted to operating and managing your practice in an efficient and cost-effective manner.

To order your copies of any of the above publications, or to enter your membership to the Economics of Law Practice Section, please see the next page.

Qty.	Title	Economics of Law Practice Members	Non-Members	Total
_____	Best of Legal Economics (5110053)	$20.00	$25.00	$_____
_____	Choosing and Using Computers (5110076)	28.00	38.00	_____
_____	Docket Control Systems (5110063).	12.00	22.00	_____
_____	Financial Management (5110045).	15.00	25.00	_____
_____	How to Avoid Being Sued (5110068)	11.00	20.00	_____
_____	How to Create-A-System for the Law Office (5110027)	20.00	25.00	_____
_____	How to Start and Build a Law Practice (5110080)	9.95†	14.95	_____
_____	Law Office Staff Manual (5110071)	18.00	28.00	_____
_____	Law Office Organization (5110079)	10.00	15.00	_____
_____	Legal Fees (5110074)	11.00	20.00	_____
_____	LOCATE (5110085)	18.00	28.00	_____
_____	Management Controls (5110049)	15.00	25.00	_____
_____	Management of a Family Law Practice (5110066)	20.00	20.00	_____
_____	Model Accounting System (5110039).	10.00	15.00	_____
_____	Model Partnership Agreement (5110072)	10.00	15.00	_____
_____	New Tricks for Old Dogs (5110048)	10.00	15.00	_____
_____	Planning for Computers (5110067)	13.00	25.00	_____
_____	Profit Planning and Budgeting (5110056)	15.00	25.00	_____
_____	Retrieval Systems (5110057)	12.00	22.00	_____
_____	Simplified Accounting Systems (5110073)	24.00	34.00	_____
_____	Style Manual (5110042).	10.00	15.00	_____
_____	Telephone Equipment (5110077)	17.00	25.00	_____
*	The Lawyer's Handbook	*	*	*
_____	Word Processing Equipment (5110051)	10.00	20.00	_____
_____	Working with Legal Assistants (5110065)	55.00	55.00	_____
_____	Your New Lawyer (5110075)	35.00	45.00	_____

* The hardbound edition of *The Lawyer's Handbook* ($45.00) may be ordered from Book Dept., ICLE, Hutchins Hall, Ann Arbor, MI 48109. Also inquire about *Law Office Information Service (LOIS)*, a comprehensive bibliography covering virtually every aspect of law firm management.

† Also includes members of Law Student Division.

Handling Charge $ 2.00

Total $_____

Name _____

Address _____

City _____ State/Country _____ Zip _____ _____

Section Membership ● Economics of Law Practice

☐ I am a member of the ABA. I have enclosed payment of $17.50 for my membership to the Section of Economics of Law Practice (which entitles me to a subscription to *Legal Economics*).

☐ I am a member of the ABA Law Student Division and have enclosed payment of $3.00 for Section membership.

To enter membership to the ABA, write to Donna Spillis at the ABA.

Name _____

Address _____

City _____ State/Country _____ Zip _____

Checks should be made payable to the American Bar Association.
Please print legibly in ink, and mail your payment with this form to the
American Bar Association, Order Fulfillment 511, 750 North Lake Shore Drive, Chicago, Illinois 60611.
Allow 4 to 6 weeks for delivery. Prices subject to change without notice.

Three "Must" Books for Lawyers & Law Students

The first three titles in the American Bar Association's Career Series are published jointly by the Law Student Division, Economics of Law Practice Section, and the Standing Committee on Professional Utilization and Career Development.

From Law Student to Lawyer: A Career Planning Manual
By Frances Utley with Gary Munneke

A detailed, step-by-step guide to career planning for the new lawyer. Describes the options, tells how to analyze individual skills and land the job.   1984 6 × 9 140 pp.

How to Start and Build a Law Practice (2nd edition)
By Jay G. Foonberg

Practical, straightforward, how-to advice on establishing a new practice—how do you get and *keep* clients, for example—or building an existing one. "It is impossible to fully do justice to this book.... It is a book that should be read and re-read...."
— *The Lawyer's Newsletter*   1984 6 × 9 256 pp.

Nonlegal Careers for Lawyers: In the Private Sector
By Frances Utley

A comprehensive survey of challenging opportunities in business and industry that utilize the skills acquired through legal training.   1984 6 × 9 104 pp.

ORDER FORM

_____ copies of *From Law Student to Lawyer* (5110081)
  ☐ $9.95   (Economics of Law Practice Section and Law Student Division members)
  ☐ $14.95 (regular price)

_____ copies of *How to Start and Build a Law Practice* (5110080)
  ☐ $9.95   (Economics of Law Practice Section and Law Student Division members)
  ☐ $14.95 (regular price)

_____ copies of *Nonlegal Careers: In the Private Sector* (5110082)
  ☐ $9.95   (Economics of Law Practice Section and Law Student Division members)
  ☐ $14.95 (regular price)

Total enclosed (add $2.00 for handling): $ _____

PAYMENT: ☐ My check or money order is enclosed.
      ☐ Charge to my account: ☐ MasterCard ☐ VISA
      Expiration date _____ / _____

      Account Number [ ][ ][ ][ ][ ][ ][ ][ ][ ][ ][ ][ ][ ][ ][ ][ ][ ]

Cardholder Signature _____

Name _____

Address_____

City/State/Zip _____

Make check payable to the American Bar Association, and mail to American Bar Association, Order Billing 511, 750 North Lake Shore Drive, Chicago, IL 60611. Allow 4 to 6 weeks for delivery.